amazon's DIRTY LITTLE SECRETS

"Whether you have an online business or operate a traditional storefront, you need to harness the amazing marketing power of the Internet that is available to every entrepreneur and small business owner. Be not afraid! The title of Greg's book, Amazon's Dirty Little Secrets, is actually lesson #1 in marketing—you have to standout and to get attention! Besides the great title, the pages of this book contain a veritable roadmap of how to attract and engage more customers and clients with email, video, and social media, often at little to no cost. Invest in this book, and more importantly, apply this information to your business."

—**Jim Palmer**, The Newsletter Guru
Author of *Stop Waiting For it to Get Easier,*
Create Your Dream Business Now, www.GetJimPalmer.com

"Greg is at the top of his game and that is very much apparent in his new book "Amazon's Dirty Little Secrets." The content is every bit as provocative as the title. This digs deeper than most surface books on the subject; the book is the one that will allow you to take action. The action you take will bring you the same actionable results that Amazon.com has used to become the world's top shopping destination. He has put so much content in here, I think I saw a kitchen sink even inside!"

—**John Lawson**, CEO ColderICE Media
Author of *Kick Ass Social Commerce for E-Preneurs@ColderICE*,
www.ColderICE.com

"As a business owner, I'm always on the lookout for a guide-book and easy-to-use checklists to help keep my brand relevant and cutting edge. I knew I could learn a lot from Amazon, including their secrets for customer retention and a remarkable customer experience, but they weren't writing a book about it. I'm so grateful for Greg Jameson's time and talent for continuing to help business owners everywhere navigate online marketing, and especially working together with others. I think that Amazon's Dirty Little Secrets is going to be a very well-used resource for me, and a go-to for helpful business topics on my radio program."

—**Angel Tuccy**
Radio Host of the *Experience Pros Radio Show,*
Denver's Longest Running Positive Business Talk Show
www.ExperiencePros.com

"Kudos to Greg Jameson on "Amazon's Dirty Little Secret." With his POWER+Plus formula, Greg provides an easy-to-follow blueprint that readers can apply to boost their Internet presence and increase their sales online.

Turn the pages and access tips and guidelines you can use to get others to market and sell for you. Among other things, Greg covers how to get traffic to your website without relying on search engines, email best practices, how to win your customers' trust, and more.

By citing specific examples, Greg illustrates how his clients have successfully implemented his advice. From search engine optimization and social media marketing to gathering testimonials and creating an engaging customer experience, he covers all the basics—not to mention, revealing "Amazon's Dirty Little Secret."

—**Debra Jason**, The Write Direction—Marketing & writing with heart, not hype, Founder of the "Freelancers' Freedom Playground"
http://writedirection.com

"The cold hard truth is the small business really cannot compete on equal footing without knowledge—the knowledge learned from books like "Amazon's Dirty Secret". The acronym POWER is a must execute plan if you want not only compete but to THRIVE. Some of Greg's advice are strategies we've done as retailers offline and were perplexed on how to apply it online. He gives you the case study on how you can do these on your online business to succeed."

—**Shirley Tan**, Author, *Ecom Hell: How to make money in Ecommerce Without Getting Burned.*
www.ecommercesystems.com

"Amazon's Dirty Little Secrets" is a wonderfully crafted manual for novice and experienced marketers alike. This book is an excellent resource, successfully pairing effective strategies with clear examples, making it easy for the reader to grasp the concepts needed to navigate the Amazon system. What makes this book even more valuable, is that the methods enclosed can be applied to any business marketing system to generate profitable results. Informative and easy to follow, this book is definitely a "must read" for every business owner.

—**Rebekah Welch**, The Marketing & Media Monsters Marketing Authors & Speakers, www.MandMMonsters.com

"Few companies so accurately predicted their future through a brand name as did Amazon.com. Bezos has created a leviathan of a business model that has retailers all over the world scrambling to compete. What many entrepreneurs don't realize is that Amazon offers amazing opportunities for authors and creators of other products to leverage the power of this giant to grow their own business. In Amazon's Dirty Little Secrets, Greg Jameson pulls back the sheet to reveal the key strategies anyone can use to tap into the marketing genius that is Amazon.com"

—**Joel Comm**, New York Times Best-Selling Author
www.JoelComm.com

I've been involved in the world of Internet marketing for years, and I am constantly searching for primers--simple tutorials that can make the complexity of the subject clear and actionable for beginners. People often ask me, "How do I approach web commerce? Where do I begin?" Finally, I can tell them: "Greg Jameson's book, 'Amazon's Dirty Little Secrets,' is all you need!"

This is the real deal, from someone who has "been there and done that." It is a practical book that tells you exactly what to do and how to do it. If you take it seriously, it is as good as any expensive course you can buy. Get this book and do what it says-- and prosper in your Internet business!

—**Dr. Joel Orr**, http://joeltrainsauthors.com

The way everyone does business has changed dramatically over the last few years: from the speed of the Internet and technology, to explosion of social media, to the demise of the economy and an uncertain future, everyone from IBM to your next door neighbor knows we all have to do things differently. But you don't have to reinvent the wheel. There are powerhouses that have figured out the new economy and, through a thorough reading and study of "Amazons Dirty Little Secrets" we can learn what we should do differently too… at least in the sense of online marketing and shared influence. I know Greg Jameson personally and have had more than one conversation where I, a Forbes & AGBeat Top Social Media Influencer, was enlightened with new ideas. I read and will re-read this book and keep it on my active (not just collectible) shelf. You'd be wise to do the same.

—**Lori Ruff**, Integrated Alliances, CEO, Speaker & Author
The Voice of www.InfluenceRadio.net

"WWJD—What would Jeff do? This mantra is one that every business owner will be repeating after reading Amazon's Dirty Little Secrets. Rather than spending hundreds, if not thousands, a month on SEO, Greg teaches you how to follow in Amazon's footsteps to build a successful marketing strategy. Greg exposes the reasons why seeking the top rank in Google doesn't need to come first in your marketing plan—or budget. Learning how to use email marketing with power partners, social media tips and tricks, and most importantly how to use Amazon's own method of having other market for you will make you a savvy marketer that can know the answer to WWJD."

—**Elizabeth Lewis, JD, MS**, Law Office of EC Lewis, PC
www.eclewis.com

Greg really lays down a plan for you in this book and walks you through everything you need to do to follow in the steps of Amazon. He uses the "Power" plan to help illustrate the key points of a successful online business. You will learn so much about everything from Search Engine Optimization, social media, affiliate marketing, e-mail marketing, and more. He has great case studies and specific tips to back up his points and a really helpful appendix on Google ranking at the end. I highly recommend this book to anyone looking to grow their online business and learn Amazon's "dirty little secret".

—**Andrea Vahl**, co-author,
Facebook Marketing All-In-One For Dummies
www.AndreaVahl.com

Amazon's Dirty Little Secret is filled with practical and proven techniques for attracting more customers and earning their loyalty. These techniques have been the driving force behind Amazon's meteoric success. The best part is you can use them to grow your business, too.

—**Ryan Healy**, Direct Response Copywriter
www.RyanHealy.com

It's not often that I find a book so worthy of recommending. "Amazon's Dirty Little Secrets" is "Meaty" and 'chock Full' of clear, concise, accurate direction and real-life examples of solid What to's and How To's. Some I've seen Only in High Level Trainings by the best in the business and others, brand new to me. I have to admit, I dug in and did my best to find flaws, but couldn't. Greg has done an excellent job simplifying and clarifying the complex. This is what's working Now. The Links are a great extension to resources and the Complete List of Google Ranking Factors is worthy of a Stand Alone Course, what a Bonus.

—Jim Zaccaria, www.JimZaccaria.com

"If you're ready to maximize your exposure and promotion so you can attract more traffic, then read and absorb the strategies in this brilliant book by Greg Jameson!"

—James Malinchak,
Featured on ABCs Hit TV Show, "Secret Millionaire"
Co-Author, Chicken Soup for the College Soul
"Two-Time National College Speaker of the Year"
Founder, www.BigMoneySpeaker.com

amazon's
DIRTY LITTLE
SECRETS

*How to Use the Power of Others
to Market and Sell for You*

Greg Jameson

NEW YORK

amazon's DIRTY LITTLE SECRETS
How to Use the Power of Others to Market and Sell for You

Published in New York, New York, by Morgan James Publishing. Morgan James and The Entrepreneurial Publisher are trademarks of Morgan James, LLC. www.MorganJamesPublishing.com

The Morgan James Speakers Group can bring authors to your live event. For more information or to book an event visit The Morgan James Speakers Group at www.TheMorganJamesSpeakersGroup.com.

A FREE eBook edition is available
with the purchase of this print book

CLEARLY PRINT YOUR NAME IN THE BOX ABOVE

Instructions to claim your free eBook edition:
1. Download the BitLit app for Android or iOS
2. Write your name in UPPER CASE in the box
3. Use the BitLit app to submit a photo
4. Download your eBook to any device

ISBN 978-1-63047-276-4 paperback
ISBN 978-1-63047-277-1 eBook
ISBN 978-1-63047-278-8 hardcover
Library of Congress Control Number:
2014940586

Cover Design by:
Rachel Lopez
www.r2cdesign.com

Interior Design by:
Bonnie Bushman
bonnie@caboodlegraphics.com

In an effort to support local communities, raise awareness and funds, Morgan James Publishing donates a percentage of all book sales for the life of each book to Habitat for Humanity Peninsula and Greater Williamsburg.

Get involved today, visit
www.MorganJamesBuilds.com.

Habitat for Humanity
Peninsula and
Greater Williamsburg
Building Partner

TABLE OF CONTENTS

INTRODUCTION

"We watch our competitors, learn from them, see the things that they were doing for customers and copy those things as much as we can."

—Jeff Bezos

The first book Amazon.com ever sold was from Jeff Bezos' garage in July 1995. The book was Fluid Concepts & Creative Analogies: Computer Models of the Fundamental Mechanisms of Thought.

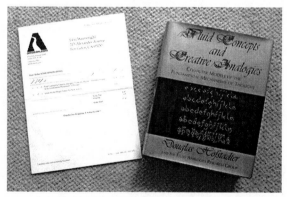

Since 1995, Amazon has established itself as the world's leader in eCommerce. Its success is not a fluke, nor is it merely the result of being in the right place at the right time.

Amazon owns 80 enormous warehouses or fulfillment centers around the globe to serve the 30 million customers that buy stuff through the portal. These warehouses are massive, with a single building taking up 1.2 million-square-feet and containing miles of conveyor belts. The logistics of running a single warehouse with millions of items are mind-boggling. On top of that, Amazon doesn't use any robots. Everything is tagged, placed and moved around by human hands. Even more amazing is the fact that Amazon doesn't store items in an organized way. Everything is stored at random, but their location tagged with barcodes. Amazon calls the system 'chaotic storage,' and this is one of the key factors to Amazon.com's success in online retail.

Essentially, a product is stored wherever there is free space, much like data is stored on a hard disk in your computer. For instance, a computer might not be with other electronics and CDs might not be with other music or media. Items are organized by barcodes and shelved by code, instead. The result is that soap may be stored next to books. It seems crazy, but it actually increases accuracy, reducing possible delivery mix-ups.

The chaotic storage system allows Amazon to utilize more shelf space and doesn't force employees to waste time organizing products. Locating items is a breeze thanks to computer-generated product lists, which help warehouse workers easily locate the specific products and prepare them for shipment.

The real advantage to chaotic storage is that it's significantly more flexible than conventional storage systems. If there are big changes in a product range, the company doesn't need to plan for more space, because the products or their sales volumes don't need to be known or planned in advance if they're simply being stored at random. Free space is also better utilized in a chaotic storage system. In a conventional system, free space may go unused for quite a while simply because stock is low or there aren't enough products. Without any kind of fixed positions, available shelf space is always being used. It's also a major time saver to not organize products as they come in. Your business may not be ready for such a storage system, but don't worry—that isn't Amazon's Dirty Little Secret.

Many people believe that Amazon's success is the direct result of a strong user shopping experience. And Amazon has become legendary for their customer service. This, however, is only part of the reason why Amazon has been the number one eCommerce company in the world for almost two decades. ***The real reason behind Amazon's success is that they have mastered the art of getting other people to market and sell for them.*** From affiliate partners that drive traffic, to online reviews and ratings where customers tell other customers why they should buy a product, Amazon is a powerhouse.

They spend millions of dollars researching what works and what doesn't work when it comes to selling products on the Internet. And in the process, they've discovered the secrets to being successful. If they have already spent all this money and figured it out, why not just copy them?

That's what this book is about—Amazon has a number of dirty little secrets about how they manage to sell more than any other etailer on the planet. In this book, I'm going to share those secrets with you. Google also has a dirty little secret about how you can get listed as number one on their search engine and remain there. I'm going to share that with you as well. In fact, I'm going to share with you the dirty little secrets of how you can energize your website for maximum sales, whether you are a small mom and pop retailer with a single location, an Internet-only shop, or a manufacturer whose business is to sell to other businesses.

Competition is fierce, especially for small shops trying to compete with Amazon or WalMart. It has been said that the Internet levels the playing field and that small businesses can compete on equal footing with large businesses, but if you are the owner of such a business you know this is not that easy. Of course when I share with you what Amazon's dirty little secrets are, you will be much further along than you were.

Marketing has changed dramatically over the past decade. People no longer read newspapers like they once did, so running an ad in the Sunday or Wednesday paper is likely to be a waste of money. But advertising on the Internet can also be a waste of money if you don't know how to do it. The dream would be that people looking for your product and services would just go to Google or Bing, enter what they are looking for, and your name would be the first (and perhaps only) choice for them to click on. But Google keeps changing the rules—how can you get to be listed number one on Google and remain there? And what if the customer doesn't know what they are looking for? One of the reasons why brick and mortar shopping overshadows Internet sales

- **O**—Offer something for free. Word of mouth is the most powerful form of marketing there is. Amazon made it big when Oprah interviewed Jeff Bezos but you can "go viral" and get others to talk about you as well. I'll give you some specific examples in this section.

- **W**—Win their trust. Amazon uses customer reviews and ratings to get others to sell products for them. This is huge! Consumers tend to trust other consumers more than they do the person selling a product, even if that person is a complete stranger. Combined with testimonials from sites like Yelp, Trip Advisor and Google reviews, you can also win your client's trust.

- **E**—Engaging experience. Amazon has the best customer experience of any website—from personalized pages and recommendations with great descriptions, lots of photos, one-click checkout, and extreme customer service, people enjoy shopping at Amazon—and they tell others about it. Learn how you can replicate this experience on your website.

- **R**—Request an action. You need to ask for the sale, but you should also request other actions, such as asking for testimonials or add-on services like a membership site.

- **+PLUS**: Perform analytics, listen to your customers, understand distribution, start now!

This book is divided into sections based upon the above POWER formula. Each section is further divided into chapters about specific topics.

P—PLENTY OF TRAFFIC

Amazon.com strives to be the eCommerce destination where consumers can find and discover anything they want to buy online.

—Jeff Bezos

his is what almost everyone talks about, from SEO to Social Media—the goal is to get more visitors to your website. All too often, most Internet marketers stop there, but this is only the first part of the equation. You might have heard people talking about "inbound marketing"—where prospects find you instead of you finding them. This has created the mindset that if you can just get to be number one on Google, it will solve all of your marketing problems, but it doesn't work that way.

You need a total Internet presence—from pay per click ads to mobile marketing—there isn't just "one thing" that works—you have to experiment with what works best for you and your organization!

The question to continually ask yourself is, "If Jeff Bezos (Amazon's founder and CEO) was running my company, WWJD"? (What Would Jeff Do?) This section provides chapters on each of these topics to help you get "Plenty of Traffic".

Search Engine Optimization

Let's address the elephant in the room first, since this is what most people ask about—SEO or Search Engine Optimization. In its simplest form, SEO is a popularity contest—the most popular sites for a particular search term are those that get listed first. I wrote a Blog post about this topic, which I'm including here. It was titled "*Why isn't my website coming up on Google?*"

This topic has been covered many times, including by me, but I continue to get asked this question. Recently I finished a brand new website for someone who does commercial photography (service changed to protect the client). The company name was Jane Doe Photos (name changed again to protect the client). Within 24 hours of the site going live, you could do a search on "Jane Doe Photos" and their site was the first one listed on Google! Not bad to go from zero presence to number one for their company name in less than a day! Most traffic from search engines for any website comes from someone searching for a particular company, not a specific product or service. In fact, the top referring keyword from Google to Amazon is "Amazon".

But the problem is that unless someone is specifically searching for "Jane Doe Photos", their site would never appear. And most likely someone is going to search for "Commercial Photography", not "Jane Doe Photos".

And this was her question. Only two weeks after her site went live, she wanted to know why she didn't come up when you did a search for "Commercial Photography" when her competitors did. The problem is of course that search engines are kind of like the chicken or the egg question—if you are driving a lot of traffic to your site, then Google will put you are the top of the list, which then drives more traffic to your site.

This was my reply:

Hi Jane Doe,

Google has over 200 variables that it uses to determine who gets listed in their results, but I'll tell you about a couple of the most important ones.

1.) The number one thing Google looks at is the number of links pointing back to your website from other websites. The keywords used in the link are a "vote" for your website for those keywords. So if you want to get listed for "commercial photography", you need to get lots of other sites pointing to your website where the link to your website is for those keywords. Here is an example:

ABC Company relies on Jane Doe for many of its <u>commercial photography projects</u>.

Notice that I'm not hyperlinking your website name, I'm using the words "commercial photography" to link to your website. If this appears on ABC Company's page, they have essentially voted for you for those keywords. The more votes you get for those keywords, the higher your placement on Google!

2.) Once someone lands on your page for a link like this, the page that the link points to needs to be about commercial photography. That is why it is critical to have written content on your pages—not just a bunch of photos. If Google follows a hyperlink and it points to page that doesn't talk about the keywords in the link, the value of that link is diminished. Each page has to contain relevant content. Your goal is not to get your site listed on the first page of Google, but rather to get each and every page listed on Google. Google doesn't rank websites, it ranks web pages.

3.) While it would be great to have all of your clients and prime contractors link to you, it turns out that you can create many of these back links to your site yourself. This is done through blogging and social media posts. All of this takes time, but you can "vote" for yourself. Besides creating these links, blogging, social media, and email campaigns also drive traffic to your website, and the amount of traffic that your website gets is another variable that Google looks at when it determines who to list on the first page. If your site has lots of links and gets lots of traffic, Google assumes it must be pretty important for the type of content you are presenting.

4.) A note about these back-links: the votes are "weighted". It turns out that it's not just the number of votes you get, but who you get them from. Kind of like the Oprah effect—a link from Oprah counts more than a link from me. A link from the American Society of Commercial Photographers site back to your site will likely be more helpful than a link from your neighbor's Facebook page. The quality of the link also matters, especially from sites that have been around a long time and a relevant to your site.

5.) This leads us to another variable that Google looks at in its page-ranking algorithm: length of time that a website has been in existence. While newer (fresh) content is perceived as more valuable than old (stale) content, websites that have been around for a long time have a higher preference than ones that were just created. There isn't much you can do here—spend the next year building back links and creating great content and you may eventually be able to pass your competitors. If you can get more votes (back-links) than your competitors, you may eventually be able to pass them, even though your site is newer.

Hopefully, this simple explanation helps you work on better placement for the pages on your website. Remember: Build lots of quality back links pointing to pages with high quality content for the keywords used to link to your page. Make sure your pages include text and not just pretty photos. Do this and the search engines will take care of themselves.

You might gather from this Blog post that I'm not a big believer in spending lots of money of SEO, and you would be correct. The primary reason is that Google keeps changing its algorithm, so it is a moving target—this leads to predatory practices by SEO companies. Even Amazon gets a "C" grade for SEO from Alexa. com. There are better ways to get traffic to your website, which we will discuss in the following chapters.

In spite of the misgivings I've described above, I've included a complete list of Google's ranking factors in the appendix. This list describes the reasons why your site might not appear in Google at all, or why it might be on page when you search for it, but on page 10 when your friend searches for it. The factors include:

Domain Factors

Factors such as domain age, whether your keywords appear in the domain name, domain registration length, domain history and who-is registration. Over 1,000 new top level domains (such as

.shop or .family) are expected to be released in 2014, it will be interesting to see how this factors into the Google algorithm.

Page-Level Factors

This includes having the keyword in the title tag, use of H1, H2, and H3 tags, keyword frequency on a page, words surrounding your keyword, page loading speed, duplicate content, image optimization, recency of content updates, magnitude of updates, outbound links, grammar and spelling, supplementary content, multimedia, internal links, broken links, reading level, affiliate links, HTML errors, JavaScript, PageRank, URLs, dynamic page variables, WordPress tags, references and sources, bullets and numbered lists, priority of page in sitemap, page age, user-friendly layout, and parked domains.

> There's a lot to take into consideration on how Google ranks your page (notice I said page, not site, because Google indexes pages, not websites—your goal should be to get every single page of your website indexed and ranked).

Site-Level Factors

Includes things such as content value, Contact Us page, domain trust, site architecture, site updates, number of pages, presence of a sitemap, site uptime, server location, SSL certificate, terms of service and privacy pages, duplicate content on site, breadcrumb navigation, mobile optimized, YouTube, site usability, use of GoogleAnalytics, user reviews and site reputation.

> YouTube videos are mentioned as a site level factor, but in fact, it is a good idea to have a YouTube video for

every single product or page for which you wish to rank. YouTube videos are given preferential treatment in the Search Engine Result Pages (SERPs) due to the fact that Google owns it. This may be the single most important thing you can do to get listed on page one of Google— create a YouTube video that is properly tagged with the keywords you wish to rank for and link back to the page on your website that the video is about. You should also embed the video on that page. For example, if you sell Christmas ornaments, create a YouTube video about each unique ornament you sell and link that video back to the ordering page for that product.

Back-Link Factors

When another site links back to your site, they are "voting" for your site. Factors that Google considers include: linking domain age, number of linking root domains, number of links from separate IP addresses, number of linking pages, Alt-tags for image links, links from .edu or .gov domains, PageRank of linking page, authority of linking domain, links from competitors, social shares of referring page, links from bad neighborhoods, guest posts, NoFollow links, diversity of link types, contextual links, sponsored links, 301 redirects, anchor text, link title, link location, link relevancy, linked to as Wikipedia source, backlink age, links from real sites versus splogs, internal or external Blog links, natural link profile, reciprocal links, user-generated content, DMOZ listed, Yahoo! Directory listed, number of outbound links, forum profile links, word count of linking content, quality of linking content, and site-wide links.

Backlinks are a significant factor in determining your search engine ranking results. But as you can see, not all links are created equal. The "anchor text" is the visible, clickable text in a hyperlink. The words contained in the anchor text can determine the ranking that the page will receive by search engines. A link that contains anchor text is more valuable than a link that just says www.MySite.com

In many cases, you can "vote" for yourself by visiting directory sites and getting your company listed with a backlink. It is important that you do this, especially with human-edited directories like DMOZ. You can also create links from blogs back to your website, which brings up the question, "Which is better, my own WordPress Blog built into my website or an external Blog hosted on blogger (which is owned by Google)?" It would make sense that a blogger site with its own domain name pointing to your primary website would provide good link juice for your site, but Google usually stops paying attention after five links from the same website pointing to your page.

Hosting a company Blog on your own website is a great way to increase traffic by providing fresh content for search engines on a daily basis. Since there is no way to host blogger on your own servers, this means all your images and video are not really yours from an SEO perspective. Rather than limiting yourself to five backlinks from a Google hosted site, your Blog should act as 'Link Bait'. Link Bait is general, useful information in a Blog format that encourages other bloggers to link to. This increases back links to the website, thus improving SEO. My recommendation is to use this approach rather than any external Blog, including blogger (even if it is owned by Google).

A further issue with the fact that Google does own blogger: Google over the past few years has taken down several of its products because they didn't want to keep supporting them, including the Google keyword tool, iGoogle and Google checkout.

When Google decides to take down blogger, you may lose all of your content that you've built up over the years. (No, I don't know when or even if Google will do this).

User-Interaction

Part of determining your site's popularity is based on how many visitors you get and how long they remain on your site. These factors include: organic click through rate for a keyword, bounce rate, direct traffic, repeat traffic, blocked sites, Chrome bookmarks, Google toolbar data, number of comments, and time spent on the site.

Special algorithm rule

Google continually tweaks its algorithm (or even completely re-writes it) to insure that it is providing relevant information to users who are searching for a particular subject matter. Factors include: query deserves freshness, query deserves diversity, user browsing history, user search history, geo-targeting, safe search, Google+ circles, DMCA complaints, domain diversity, transactional searches, local searches, Google News Box, Big Brand preference, shopping results, image results, and single site results for brands.

These special algorithm rules are part of the reason why different users get different results when searching for the same keyword. Local searches (based on your physical location), combined with your past search history and browsing history influence the results that are displayed.

People often ask, "Does Google punish sites that don't pay them for PPC ads by lowering their rankings, thus encouraging participation in AdWords where Google makes money?" The answer is No. Always has been and always will be. The simple reason is that doing this would reduce the relevance of Google's main organic rankings. And once that happens, Bing or another search engine will unseat them as the Big Dog of search. You can't buy your way into the organic results, but at the same time, the Internet is no longer a level playing field. As mentioned, one of the ranking factors is a preference for big brands. Little guys have a harder time trying to compete (unless you use Amazon's Dirty Little Secret of leveraging others to market and sell for you!)

Social Signals

Social media plays an increasingly important factor on search engine results. Some of things Google considers are: number of tweets, authority of Twitter users accounts, number of Facebook likes, Facebook shares, authority of Facebook user accounts, Pinterest Pins, LinkedIn connections, votes on social sharing sites, number of Google +1's, authority of Google+ user accounts, verified Google+ authorship, social signal relevancy, and site-level social signals.

If you do not have a strong social media presence, this may impact your ability to place well in the search results. In fact, several of the 10 most important factors in SEO ranking now come from social media, with Google +1s leading the way.

Brand Signals

The strength of your brand impacts the search engine results as well including: brand name anchor text, branded searches, Facebook Page and likes, Twitter profile and followers, official LinkedIn company page, employees listed at LinkedIn, legitimacy of social media accounts, brand mentions on news sites, co-citations, number of RSS subscribers, brick and mortar location with Google+ local listing, and if your website is a tax-paying business.

On-site Webspam Factors

Some of the on-site factors that can negatively affect your search placement include: Panda Penalty, Links to bad neighborhoods, redirects, popups or distracting ads, site or page over-optimization, ads above the fold, hiding affiliate links, affiliate sites, auto-generated content, excess PageRank sculpting, IP address flagged as spam, and meta tag spamming.

Off-page Webspam Factors

Some of the off-site factors that can impact your search placement in a negative way include: unnatural influx of links, Penguin Penalty, link profile with high percentage of low quality links, linking domain relevancy, unnatural links warning, sinks from the same class C IP, "poison" anchor text (like Cialis or Viagra), manual penalties, selling links, Google Sandbox, Google Dance, disavow tools and reconsideration requests.

As you can see, there are hundreds of factors that affect where you will show up in the search results for a particular search phrase. Is it any wonder that the commercial photographer example I gave at the beginning of this chapter didn't show up? The most important things you can do are:

1. Create original, quality content that your readers want to consume. You may have noticed that written words are more important than photos (although original photos tagged with alt text may also be consumed by your readers). That's because Google can easily read your written content.

2. Get lots of high quality sites linking back to your site, preferably with the anchor text containing the keywords you wish to rank for, and

3. Use Google properties such as YouTube and Google+ to create links yourself. Supplement these with other links that you can also control such as directories, blogs, article sites, review sites and coupon sites.

Here are a couple of tools you can use to see how your website stacks up to these variables:

http://developers.google.com/speed/pagespeed/insights/
http://www.woorank.com/

As I mentioned before, Google keeps changing the rules, so even if you show up on page one today, you might not even appear at all in a week. This can be frustrating to Internet marketers. *So what do you do about it? Don't rely on search engines for your traffic!* If Google sends traffic your way, that's great, but it should be icing on the cake. The bulk of your traffic should come from things you can control by driving traffic to your site yourself! We'll talk more about some ways you can do this in the remaining chapters of this section.

"YOU, not Google, are responsible for driving traffic to your website."

—Greg Jameson

Email

Email is the single best way to drive traffic to your website. And while Amazon does this better than most, that is not their real dirty little secret.

We saw in the last chapter that while many people think that getting listed on page one of Google is the best way to drive traffic to your website, it is not reliable. In fact, it isn't even the best way to get traffic—email is. Search and social have long been touted as the dynamic duo in marketing, but data from Monetate's Ecommerce Quarterly report shows email is the biggest driver of conversions. In analyzing more than 500 million shopping experiences, Monetate found the conversion rate for email marketing was more than 3 percent, while search came in under 2 percent and social under 1 percent. But conversions weren't the only area where email shined. Email rivaled search as a top referrer leading to the most page views on a site, about 9 pages per visitor.

The reason why email performs so well is because people have either opted in to your list, or because someone they know has emailed them on your behalf (word of mouth). I'll discuss more about this in the next section of the book (O—Offer something for free).

Of course, like search, email is also a chicken or the egg scenario—how can you email to a large number of people and get them to visit your site if you don't have a large list?

SPAM

Because email works so well, it causes problems, namely spam. If email weren't so effective at driving people to websites, there wouldn't be so much unwanted email. Here is what has happened:

- Approximately 5 million spam-sending botnets worldwide.
- On average, a single botnet sends 77 emails per minute.
- 88% of all spam is sent from botnets.
- 70 spam emails received by the average web user each day (McAfee)

That's a problem by itself, but one-third of permission e-mails that consumers want to receive from trusted sources are being blocked by e-mail filters and corporate firewalls due to the problem of spam.

The CANSPAM Act was passed in 2003 in an attempt to stop the email problem. It stands for: Controlling the Assault of Non-Solicited Pornography and Marketing.

This law tells us what you can't do:

- Deceptive email headers
- Deceptive subject lines
- Not giving opt-out
- Not providing your physical mailing address
- Make multiple accounts to send email
- Send fraudulent, obscene, or child porn

It also states what you can do:

- Email people without permission (as long as not dictionary style list)
- Send multiple emails until someone opts out
- Send commercial email

Notice that you are permitted to email someone without their permission. In spite of what you may have heard, you can buy a list (as long as that list has been legally collected) and you can email to that list. A list that has been developed by researching websites and manually mining email address from websites that publically display an email address on a "Contact Us" page is fair game. When someone has provided their email address to a company and that company's policies ask them if they want to receive offers from other "partners", their email address is also fair game.

For example, if you exhibit at a tradeshow, and the tradeshow management provides you with a list of attendees to the show, you may legally email them, even if they did not specifically ask to be on your list. If you have a physical store and collect email addresses on customer receipts, you can email to them. If you have an Internet store and collect email addresses as part of the checkout process (which all stores do), you can email to those customers even if they don't further optin to a list. If you collect business cards at a networking event, you may email to those people. The law allows you to do this.

Still, most email service providers such as Constant Contact, iContact, MailChimp, AWeber, etc. will blacklist you if you send emails to anyone who has not specifically opted-in to your list. Many require you to have a double opt-in, where the person provides you with their email address, then specifically responds to a confirmation email asking them if they really want to be on your email list. However, this is only to protect themselves from complaints—it is not required by law.

Basically, the rules are as follows:

- The CAN-SPAM Act allows direct marketing email messages to be sent to anyone, without permission, until the recipient explicitly requests that they cease ("opt-out").
- Every message must include opt-out instructions. The sender must honor the opt-out requests of recipients within 10 days. An email recipient cannot be required to pay a fee, provide information other than his or her email address and opt-out preferences, or take any steps other

than sending a reply email message or visiting a single Internet Web page to opt out of receiving future email from a sender.

- A valid physical postal address is required. A PO Box satisfies this requirement.

Grow your list

OK, so just because you are allowed to email to anyone and everyone until they opt-out doesn't mean that you should. And the reason why you shouldn't has nothing to do with legal or moral reasons. It's because those people may not be interested in what you are offering in the first place. Why waste your time sending out emails to someone who doesn't care and is only going to get mad that you keep emailing them when they are not interested. Often the emails are never opened or worse, they bounce back, flooding your own in-box and sending negative signals to your email service provider.

You want to build up a primary list of emails where your recipients not only want to hear from you, but are excited and expecting to hear from you. You want people on your list that when you don't send them an email, they send you one asking why they haven't heard from you!

How do you get these emails in the first place?

The way most people will tell you to collect emails is to have a form on your website asking for people to opt-in to your list. But *why* would someone do this? And if you aren't getting much traffic in the first place, this is going to be a very slow process for building up a sizeable list, as you would be relying on search to drive people to your website in the first place. As we've seen, this won't create a quantum leap for you, at least not anytime soon. Besides, you need to be careful how you collect email addresses. Many times in online forms or other sign-ups, people will provide bogus email addresses that, when you send email to them, will generate hard bounces and appear to the ISP as irresponsible sending.

Marketing is hard and expensive. Amazon's Dirty Little Secret (as you'll learn more about later) is to let other people do it for you! While Amazon today might not need others to email on their behalf, they grew their business by letting affiliates sell for them in the first place. And over 40% of Amazon's sales today are still derived from affiliates!

The point is, if you don't have a large email list, find someone who does and let them email on your behalf! This is what is known as "joint ventures".

Perhaps the most difficult thing to do in this business is to create a loyal following of paying clients... from scratch. It's so difficult, in fact, that I don't recommend you put a lot of effort into it. Instead, try asking yourself this simple question...

"Who already has access to large numbers of my ideal clients?"

You can segment this question into three questions that might help you find your ideal JV partners:

- What do my ideal clients buy... BEFORE buying from me?
- What else does my Specific Audience buy...WHILE buying from me?
- What does my Specific Audience buy... immediately AFTER buying from me?

For example, if you sell Christmas ornaments and decorations, why not create a joint venture partnership with a Christmas tree supplier? If you sell exercise clothing, how about partnering with someone who sells exercise equipment? Perhaps you sell services like horse training—why not partner with a feed store. Are you starting to see some possibilities for your business?

Now that you've determined who already has access to the people you want to sell to, you must determine what you can do to add value to those prospective JV partners. For example, if you are selling handmade belt buckles, you might find someone who is selling handmade leather belts. The relationship is obvious—the company with the belts sends out an email to their customers about your buckles. Because the readers already have a relationship with the belt maker, they trust his/her opinions and look at your offer.

But here is the important part: *the offer has to make sense to both the buyer **and the JV partner.*** Just because the offer is good for the buyer isn't enough—you must have an incentive for the belt maker to send these emails for you in the first place. You must compensate the JV partner strongly enough that they will want to do the marketing for you. Often this involves giving them a cut of every sale made. For many products, this might be as much as 50% of the gross profit (cost of the item less cost to manufacture—for digital downloads that is just 50% of the price).

Your joint venture does not have to be based on selling a physical product or service. You may be putting on a seminar, webinar or podcast and need to get attendees—if you can provide a good reason for someone with a larger list to promote your event, this can work well as a way of letting someone else market and sell for you.

Email Best Practices—What Would Jeff Do?

Now that you've built your list, how can you effectively communicate with your subscribers? Since this is a book about

Amazon's Dirty Little Secrets, let's consider how Amazon looks at email marketing:

Target your subscribers

Your list should be segmented, based on who the customer is and what they've purchased from you in the past. Amazon again does a great job of this—I get emails from them based upon things I've both purchased and things I've looked at but have not purchased. I have never gotten an email from them asking me to buy something I'm not interested in.

Of course, you can segment your list based upon geography, frequency or amount of purchase, how their name got added to your list, or anything else you know about that person. The point is to make the emails personal and relevant. Track absolutely everything your customers do. When it comes to running an online business, data is power. Remember, you can never segment your customers enough.

TEST

Never send an email without first testing it. A test should involve several things: First, test it on yourself, just to make sure it renders the way you expect it to when you actually receive the email. Next, test it on a few friends, asking for their input. Finally, run a test on a small portion of your list (about 100 people)— usually to 2 or more groups with something different for each group, such as the subject line or the call to action. From this you can determine which email performs the best. Based on this information, you can now send the best performing email to the rest of your list segment.

One thing Amazon does well is setting up series of emails. They're not afraid to email their customers. Always A/B test your email campaigns for frequency but in general there are opportunities to maximize your returns if you get the frequency right. You should not only send an email a few hours after a customer abandons the cart but another 24 hours after that. This can increase your conversions by 20% or more, just by adding a second email. Here is an example of an email I received from Amazon after not completing an order:

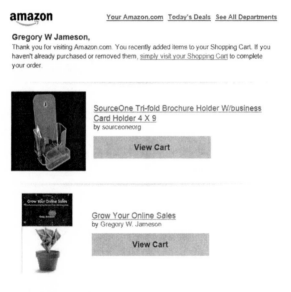

Encourage click-throughs without making the customer think

Make sure that there is a call to action on the email that encourages someone to click on the link. Emails with too many different links are not likely to get clicked on. Keep your emails to a single subject and don't link out to more than 2 or 3 individual products. You want to make it easy for the customer to view your offer and decide to click.

Making the user experience as simple as possible is an important step in maximizing conversions from your email marketing. This can extend from simply calling the customer by their first name to automatically logging customers in anytime they are required to return to your site. When you visit Amazon.com, no matter which email you receive, which link you click or even if you just visit the site directly, you can always view your shopping cart, add to it, and remove from it, etc. without re-authenticating. Provide a single call to action—Amazon's emails are generally very specific and direct.

Optimize for mobile

A large and growing percentage of people now open their emails primarily or at least first on their mobile devices. You need to make sure that your email is read rather than deleted. Simple text-based emails with only small images (that are not critical to the message) work best for mobile devices. When you do your testing, be sure to read the email on a mobile device to see how it will render.

Personalize your emails

People like getting emails that are addressed to them, not "Dear Customer". They also appreciate getting emails that are from someone, not a company. Sign your name to your emails!

Personalizing emails can certainly increase your conversions. But be careful! As Seth Godin says:

> Dear <first name> is far worse than no mailmerge at all. Here's the simple test: if you're not willing to spend fifteen seconds per name reviewing the list and cleaning it up (why did you email me six times?), then don't expect

that we have fifteen seconds to read what you wrote. If you have 4,000 names, that's 1,000 minutes. Don't have 1,000 minutes? Don't send the mail.

Text is what humans send. Corporations send HTML and pretty graphics. Either can work if expectations are set properly, but if you're a human, act like one.

Why are you emailing me? If you can't tell me in six words what you need me to do, it's unlikely I'll be able to guess.

If your email promotion is a taking, not a giving, I think you should rethink it. If you still want to take the time and attention and trust of your 4,000 closest friends, think hard about what that means for the connections you've built over the years. There are few promotional emergencies that are worth trading your reputation for.

Consider how often and when to send

Believe it or not, if you don't send enough emails, people will stop thinking about you and/or think you don't have anything useful to provide. I've gotten up to 3 emails a day from some companies, which I find annoying—in fact 1 email a week might even be annoying to some. But one email a week is certainly not intrusive, and if you only send one email a month, you are likely not maximizing your email marketing.

Capitalize on Current Events

Current events can be powerful for any of your marketing—from social media to press releases. The same is true with your emails. Consider this email I received from Amazon:

How can you relate your emails to current events?

Be consistent: email is an extension of your store

Think of email as giving you a chance to bring your store to the customer in their inbox. Amazon nails this. Keeping their email content and templates consistent, not only with each other but with their website itself. Widgets within emails (such as the product recommendation widget below) look and feel just like they would on their website. By keeping their campaign designs and content consistent with their overall store they create a holistic experience for their customers. This in turn leads to familiarity, which builds trust and trust is always a good thing.

Don't just send discounts or offers.

Your store has a myriad of aspects. Just some of the emails you receive from Amazon regularly include newsletters, cart abandonment reminders, special competitions, requests for reviews, random product recommendations, reminders to sign up for Amazon Prime, etc. In most cases Amazon does not offer discounts—bear this in mind. You generally don't discount everything in your store, so don't do so in emails you send out.

Email your customers after they order from you as well as trying to get them to order. For example, on the next page is an email I received from Amazon after ordering a part for my dryer.

Notice the call to action, asking me to review the purchase I made. The email is personalized as well.

Retain customers with clever unsubscribe options

Unsubscriptions are a part of email marketing campaigns. Ultimately you want uninterested customers to unsubscribe. It does you no good to be emailing customers who don't want to receive your messaging so you should always make unsubscribing easy.

By giving your customers options you also open the door to increase retention. Customers unsubscribe for a variety of reasons. It could be the volume of emails you're sending, specific content

amazon.com

Hi Gregory W Jameson, will you please take a minute to share your experience?

You Purchased:

Whirlpool 8573069 Element for Dryer (New)
Seller note: In stock ready to ship!

From Seneca River Trading, Inc.
Estimated Delivery Date: November 20, 2013 - November 27, 2013

How did the seller do?

<u>Excellent</u> - Item delivered on time, was as described, great customer service (if contacted)
<u>**I had a different experience...**</u>

Does the product meet your expectations?
Rate and Review Purchases

Helpful Links
View Order Details | Contact the Seller | View Seller Profile | Feedback Help

or just the channel. Bear these in mind when thinking about your unsubscribe process.

Use subtle psychology

Amazon is pretty clever when it comes to understanding their customers and they try all sorts of tactics to get conversions. They use urgency to get people to act. They also recognize that customers may be looking for something other than what they have previously browsed or purchased. Try putting yourself in the mind of the customer in order to drive maximum conversions.

YouTube

My dryer recently quit working. It was running, but it wasn't generating any heat. Not being an appliance repairman, but deciding to save some money, I did a search on Google for my model number and "not heating", and discovered it could be one of three things: the heating element, the thermostat, or the thermo fuse. Google also displayed the results of YouTube videos that showed me how to change these parts myself.

There was a great 3 minute video showing me how easy it was to replace the part I needed, combined with a short description of the video that had a link to a page where I could buy that exact part.

That is the power of YouTube! You may have heard that YouTube is the number 2 search engine behind Google (ahead of Bing or Yahoo), but here's the thing: YouTube is owned by Google, so videos posted on YouTube are displayed in the Google Search results.

As we discussed in chapter one, everyone who has a website wants to get listed number one on Google. This seems to be the Holy Grail of Internet marketing. But Google is always changing the rules, purposefully trying to mix it up so that their site is dynamic. How then can you get to be number one on Google and remain there? This is Google's dirty little secret—it's called YouTube.

What most business owners don't understand is that having videos is the single best way to get your site listed on the first page of the Google results. Here's a tip: Google likes to use their own web properties to feed search results. If you haven't claimed your spot on places.google.com or Google+, do it. Then go make yourself a video and post it on YouTube.

You don't have to pay a SEO (Search Engine Optimization) company tens of thousands of dollars or use Google AdWords to get listed number one on Google. You just need to have enough content out there that Google thinks you are important. And having a video is the best way to do that. Let me show you an example:

I have a client that sells imported items at wholesale. One of the more popular items they distribute is ironwood figures that are imported from the Seri Indians in Mexico. If you did a search on "ironwood figures", their site did not come up at all in Google. So I created a short 2 minute video about ironwood figures and posted it on YouTube. In the description of the video, I added a link to the page on their website for ironwood figures. (You can add a link on YouTube by entering the complete URL starting with http://). Within days, that YouTube video was showing up on the first page of Google for the search term "ironwood figurines". More importantly, within a week their website was showing up on page one of Google for that search term. Amazingly, without doing any other form of search engine optimization, both the video and their webpage remain on page one of Google 3 years later!

This worked so well, that this same company asked me to do another video on another one of their product lines—Pakistan baskets. It was the exact same scenario: they were not being index or ranked at all for the term "Pakistan baskets". And again, both the video and their website now show up on page one of Google for this search term and have remained there for over 3 years!

Was this a fluke? I did some further experiments, this time with a small local company called Parker Feed Store. Parker Feeds sells horse feed and pet supplies, but a large chain store moved in *right across the street* from them that was a direct competitor. To make matters worse, if you did a Google search for "Parker Feed Store" (the name of their business), the competitor's site came up, and Parker Feeds did not show up at all. So I built them a short 2 minute video and posted it on YouTube. Again, I linked back to their site in the description. And sure enough, both the video and their site are now on page one of Google (and their competitor is not!)

I have repeated this process for multiple clients. The result is not always a page one listing, but without exception, it has always improved their page ranking.

Next, you have to have a catchy title. I released another video that became popular called "Amazon's Dirty Little Secret". If I had called this video "Using Customer Reviews and Ratings to Drive Sales", it probably would have gotten 10% of the views that it did, simply because the title wouldn't have been as compelling. Titles matter—make yours be something that attracts attention if you want your video to get viewed.

But it turns out that you don't have to have a lot of views for your video to get your website to the number one slot on Google. You just have to have one. It DOES have to be properly tagged with appropriate keywords and have a description that also uses those keywords. The description MUST have a link back to your website. To do this, include the full URL including http://www.yourwebsite.com. The http:// is required.

Now that you have your video uploaded to YouTube, embed it on the appropriate page of your website. For example, if your video is about how to properly select a saddle for your horse, embed this video on the page of your site that sells saddles.

Remember how I said you should claim your space at places.google.com. Now go back to those sites and attach your video to your profiles. At this point, you have a single video that you uploaded one time to YouTube, but it links back to your site, it is embedded on your site, and it is attached to your other Google profile properties. Google thinks you are a rock star, and you are 50% more likely to get listed on page one and stay there! And if you commit to doing one video per month for 12 months, you will be ahead of 75% of the eCommerce sites out there. So the secret is out—video will make you an expert and Google will love you.

Facebook

Why does Facebook get its own chapter, when all the other social media sites are grouped together in the next chapter? Just like Google is the king of search engines, Facebook is the dominant player in social media. Regardless of whether you are a B2B or a B2C company, you simply must have a business page on Facebook. But just like everything else, simply having a page is not enough—you have to work it on a regular basis and you have to get people to engage with you in order to make it effective.

In the introduction, I mentioned how Oreo cookies have more likes on their Facebook page than either Google or Amazon. In fact, as of this writing, Oreo has over 35 million likes, Amazon has 22 million and Google 15 million. How is this possible—a single product (a hard cookie with questionable "white stuff" holding it together), outshines two of the world's biggest brands that have numerous products? The answer lies in engagement with the customer. Rihanna has over 82 million likes on her page—and for the same reason. The same goes for Lady Gaga with 61 million likes. She is a single product that knows how to engage with her audience.

Of course, all of those are big brands or big celebrities. What happens to the little guy? In the past, Facebook encouraged small companies to create a business page then get "fans" to "like" your page. The concept remains valid—you create a page for your business and keep those posts separate from your person profile. That way you can post personal messages to your family and friends, and you can post business messages to your business page. This also made sense from another perspective—Facebook only allows you to have 5,000 personal friends, but an unlimited number of fans who like your page.

This worked—for a while. But the problem is that too many companies created pages and too many people liked those pages. In order to keep the Facebook timeline under control and relevant to the user, Facebook created its own algorithm called "EdgeRank". EdgeRank determines which stories appear in a user's news feed. The first thing someone sees when they log into Facebook is the news feed. This is a summary of what's been happening recently among their friends on Facebook. The EdgeRank algorithm hides boring stories, so if your story doesn't score well, no one will see it. Consider this image:

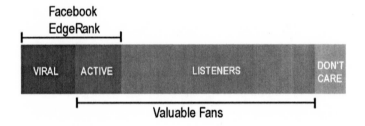

Here's the problem with Facebook's philosophy, at least as far as your business is concerned: on a day to day basis, the listeners are the ones who drive the majority of value to you. It's just like a Blog post where lots of people might read it, but only a few comment on it. Today, EdgeRank filters out 84% of your fans, simply because they are listeners, rather than active engagers. These are people who decided to follow you, but are not filtered out because they rarely engage. But they don't want to engage, they just want to listen to what you have to say! That's pretty bad—84% of you audience lost just because Facebook decided to filter them out (and make you pay for the privilege of showing up on their newsfeed).

As the owner of a business Facebook page, you used to be able to email your fan base, but Facebook probably took that away because it didn't make them any money. Now they are taking away organic reach of your posts. Melanie Dodaro wrote a Blog post called "Is Facebook Organic Reach Dead?" where she claims that organic reach of your Facebook posts is now less than 2%.

Stories from your friends typically appear within your newsfeed, sprinkled with a few stories from the pages you've "liked". But you only have about a 2% chance of showing up in someone's newsfeed if you are posting on your page, compared to about a 90% chance of posting as yourself on your own timeline. And it's getting worse—views from organic Facebook Page posts have been declining. A recent announcement from Facebook explains why.

"On a given day, when someone visits News Feed, there are an average of 1,500 possible stories we can show," says Facebook. "Because the content in News Feed is always changing, and we're seeing more people sharing more content, Pages will likely see changes in distribution."

What this means is that posts you create on your business page are basically never getting seen by your fans. The only way to get these posts to appear is to either:

- Pay Facebook in the form of a promoted post or sponsored story, or
- Have your post "go viral" by getting lots of people to "like", "share", or "comment" on it.
- Post as an individual to your friends, and forget about your business posts.

The last one is not really an option for many business owners. So what can you do?

What This Means for Merchants

Facebook has been reluctant to admit that advertising is the best way to get Page content noticed. However, a recent Facebook document entitled, "Generating business results on Facebook" leaves little room for doubt that organic placement is no longer sufficient to grow a fan base or gain visibility in News Feed.

Facebook now says advertising is the only way to guarantee News Feed visibility.

"We expect organic distribution of an individual Page's posts to gradually decline over time as we continually work to make sure people have a meaningful experience on the site," the document said.

Facebook's solution to this problem: advertise.

"To maximize delivery of your message in News Feed, your brand should consider using paid distribution, as it enables you to reach people beyond your fan base and move beyond the organic competition," stated the document.

8 Tips for Merchants

Based on Facebook's own words, to get content seen by the most people, Page owners will have to advertise. Because people spend more than 50 percent of their time on the News Feed, ads that appear there stand a much better chance of garnering attention. According to Facebook, ads in the News Feed get a 96 percent greater return on ad spend than those in the right-hand column.

Aside from that, here are eight tips for merchants to maximize the value of organic posts.

1. **Make posts timely and relevant.** The more relevant the content, the more likely people are to engage with it. Before posting, ask yourself, "Would people share this with their friends or recommend it to others?"

2. **Add value to your readers.** Give readers behind-the-scenes insights into your business, share interesting tips on using your products, and post relevant third-party content such as links to interesting articles or customer testimonials.

3. **Include the use of photos.** Kissmetrics, an analytics platform, reports that posts containing photos get 53 percent more Likes, 104 percent more comments, and 84 percent more clicks than those that do not. So, when possible use photos. Better yet, create a "Facebook Store" using photo albums to arrange images about the products you sell, then add links in the photo descriptions to the product pages of your eCommerce website. I give a detailed explanation about how to do this in my book "Grow Your Online Sales".

4. **Use simple, short copy.** This helps ensure fans read the entire message. Kissmetrics says that posts with less than 80 characters get 66 percent more engagement.

5. **Create content that targets specific audience segments.** This helps to ensure content has relevance and speaks to the interests of those targeted.

6. **Pay attention to Page statistics.** Insights, the analytics component tied to Pages, can help you see which posts are driving the most engagement, views, and reach. With this knowledge you can post more of the same. Also, pay attention to the day of the week, time of day,

and frequency of posts, as this will help you optimize posting activity.

7. **Encourage engagement.** Ask questions, use polls and "fill in the blank" posts to stimulate engagement from fans. End posts with a call to action asking them to comment, Like, and share.

8. **Interact with fans and others.** Reply to people who comment on posts with a comment of your own, and thank those who Like or share your content. This lets them know you are paying attention.

Increasing Engagement

RSS Feed

Even if you do all of the above, unless you advertise on Facebook, you somehow need to reach your fans, so they will help you make your posts go viral. Since Facebook isn't showing your posts to your fans, perhaps you can get them to subscribe to the RSS Feed of your Facebook page. What's that you say—there's an RSS feed for my page? Yes—here's how to find it:

Go to your page and copy the page URL to your clipboard. For example, https://www.facebook.com/WebStoresLtd

Now go to FindMyFacebookID.com. Paste in the URL and click on Lookup numeric ID.

Enter your personal Facebook profile URL:

https://www.facebook.com/WebStoresLtd

Lookup numeric ID...

Copy the numeric id to your clipboard.

Success! If your name is *WebStores Ltd*, then we found your numeric ID:

106187753111

Now go to: www.facebook.com/feeds/page.php?format=atom10&id=XXX

Where xxx=your numeric id.

You should now be on a standard feed page—send this to all of your fans and try to get them to subscribe to your Facebook posts so they never miss another. Then ask them to comment and share your posts. You can only do this for pages, not personal timelines. That's ok because friends still see your personal posts—this is so you can get your page in front of your fans. Of course you can do this for pages you want to follow as well.

Of course you can, and should be integrating your Facebook marketing with your other marketing efforts as well such as email and print media.

Embedded Posts

Another great way to increase engagement with your Facebook page is to use embedded posts. Embedded Posts are a simple way to put public posts—by a Page or a person on Facebook—into the content of your website or web page. Only public posts from Facebook Pages and profiles can be embedded. Here's how:

Find the post you want to embed on your web page or Blog.

Click on the down arrow in the upper right of the post, then click on "Embed Post". A screen appears with some code.

Copy the code to your clipboard, then paste it into the code area of your web page or post.

Because of the way that Facebook is no longer displaying your posts to your fans, you can expose it to a larger audience — one that probably didn't see the original post on Facebook—by adding the post to a popular Blog post. Embedded posts are live links so they count just like additional exposure on Facebook.

Tabs / Apps / Sign-up Form

Facebook allows you to add custom tabs to your business pages, which can include a framed page from your website. That is, you can put any page from your website (even one that doesn't appear on your website navigation) and make it available to your Facebook fans or visitors. This makes it possible to actually sell something on Facebook or provide a form to sign up for your emails. While traffic to your page is even less than the number of people that see your posts on the newsfeed, I still recommend that you add custom tabs and apps to engage with your audience. This can be useful for growing your email list.

Case Study

I recently received a postcard in the mail from the YMCA of the Rockies. It contained a punch-out "fan" with a picture of Sampson the Elk on it, with instructions that if you took a picture of yourself holding the "Gratitude Elk", you would be eligible for a drawing for a 2 night stay at the YMCA. This is a great way to attract visitors to your Facebook Page and actually have them engage with you. Here's how it worked:

First you had to Like their page in order to be able to enter the contest. This is known as a "fangate".

Once you had liked their page, then you could look at the other entries or submit your own entry. You could also offer something for free, such as an eBook. In this case, the YMCA asked you to submit a photo of yourself with the postcard they sent you in order to be including in their drawing.

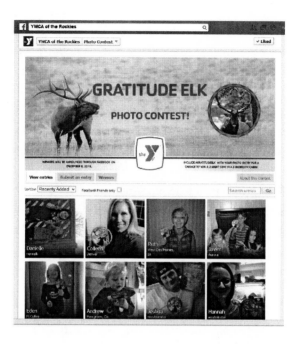

I don't know how many entries they actually received, but they gave away something for free of significant value (2 night stay in a 3 bedroom cabin), and they got lots of people to interact with their page.

Following the YMCA example, here's a secret, unadvertised special: you can get the price you paid for this book back 4X! Just take a picture of yourself reading this book in an unusual place (at an airport, on a ski lift, at the beach—whatever). Post it on Facebook and tag "Greg Jameson" in the photo so I can see that you did this. Then I will send you a code to the WebStores VIP Membership site that is good for one month (a $97 value).

Another option, which the YMCA may have also used (but I didn't see it), would be to advertise your special behind the fangate. For example, if you are offering a free eBook, you could set up a fangate that would require someone to like your page, then they would have the opportunity to download your eBook, which you can use to drive traffic to your website.

Images on Facebook

You may have heard (or seen) that pictures can drive big engagement on Facebook. According to Facebook, images receive 120 percent more engagement than text-only posts.

This is great news for any small business that's been struggling to get people to like, comment, or share, but also introduces a whole new question: How can I use images in my Facebook marketing?

Here are dozen ideas to get your creative juices flowing:

1. **Celebrate your customers**

   Celebrating your customers builds strong relationships and markets your products and services in a whole new way. You can also tag your customers in your photos and thank them for stopping by.

2. **Show fans what they missed**

   Next time you have an event, make sure to take plenty of photos. You can then share those photos on Facebook and give attendees the opportunity to tag themselves after the event. For people who missed the event, photos offer a big incentive to put future events on their calendar.

3. **Help support a good cause**

   People like to spend money with businesses that share the same values and support the same causes. They also like to share information regarding those values and causes. Images will be sure to inspire your fans to get involved.

4. **Show off your accolades**

   Don't be modest! If you receive a great piece of coverage or an endorsement from an influencer in your industry, share it with your fans on Facebook.

5. **Drive people to your Blog**

   If you manage a Blog for your business, you know that generating traffic to your content can often be a challenge. If you haven't already, try to use a fun and engaging photo to encourage people to click-through.

6. **Encourage people to share the love**

   There's a reason why the people who" Like" your Facebook Page are known as fans. These are the people who know your business, appreciate the work that you do, and are happy to show their support. Encouraging them to show the love on sites like Yelp can have a big impact when it comes to boosting your online reputation and bringing new customers to your business.

7. **Show what people can do with your products**

   If you're a restaurant, bakery, or caterer, using pictures to show off all of the great stuff coming out of your kitchen is sure to boost engagement. When you're a fabric store, there are endless possibilities of what customers can create with the stuff you sell. Showing customers some examples of how they can use your products will inspire your audience and can often generate quite a conversation.

8. **Have some fun**

   Don't forget, Facebook is supposed to be fun for you and more importantly for your customers. A "caption this" or "fill in the blank" contest are both great ways to engage your fans and have some fun in the process.

9. **Tap into current events**

   While there are certainly hot topics and current events you'll want to avoid, many events are a great chance to use photos to boost engagement on your Facebook Page. Just make sure you're staying true to your brand and keeping the interest of your fans in mind!

10. **Say thanks**

    Don't underestimate the power of a simple "thank you." Add a photo of your staff to provide a more personal touch.

11. **Help get people through your door**

    "Sell! Sell! Sell!" isn't a strategy that's going to work on Facebook. If you want to get people off of Facebook and into your store, you need to provide a more personal touch. Free treats and a relaxed shopping experience will work better.

12. **Let people know where to find you**

    If you manufacture products that can be found in other locations, you can use Facebook to let people know where to find you. If your products are available at other local retailers, you can tag the business in your Facebook post.

Other Social Media Sites

Quite honestly, Amazon doesn't participate very actively in most social media sites, primarily following their philosophy of letting other do it for them. That isn't to say that Amazon doesn't have a social media presence, just that for their size, they don't do as much as many smaller companies (and may be the reason why Oreo cookies has more fans). For example, unlike most sites on the Internet today, Amazon does not display icons on its site linking to their pages on Facebook, Twitter, or LinkedIn. They do have "share" links that allow others to post to Twitter or Facebook on their behalf. (Copy this technique from Amazon as well and display share icons on *your* site so others can spread the word for you!)

While Facebook is the dominant player when it comes to social media, your business might benefit by participating in other forms of social media as well. Here are some others.

YouTube

We already discussed YouTube—most people today are aware that it is the number 2 search engine on the Internet, but did you know that YouTube is also a social media site? You can post comments on any YouTube video and engage with others. People can follow you by subscribing to your channel. YouTube is a great place to engage with your customers.

Here is the link to Amazon's YouTube channel:

http://www.youtube.com/user/Amazon

Here is the link to my WebStores Ltd channel:

http://www.youtube.com/user/WebStoresLtd

And the link to the video, "Amazon's Dirty Little Secret", which was the inspiration behind this book:

http://www.youtube.com/watch?v=RoSEiO1JfSE

Blogs

Yes, blogs are actually considered a type of social media, in that your readers can (and should) comment on your posts and create a conversation. A big advantage of blogs is that people can follow you through an RSS feed. Plus, companies that Blog generate 67% more leads per month than those who don't according to HubSpot.

While they don't promote their blogs, Amazon actually has two:

SES (Simple Email Service) Blog: http://sesblog.Amazon.com/

AWS (Amazon Web Services Blog): http://aws.typepad.com/aws/

And here is the link to my Blog:
http://webstoresltd.com/Blog/

If you'd like to follow me through an RSS feed, here is the link:
http://webstoresltd.com/feed/

Twitter

Twitter is a "real-time" social media site, consisting largely of short 140 character posts that, due to the size limitation, are usually just a bunch of links. For example, here is Amazon's Twitter page:

https://Twitter.com/Amazon

This is a typical tweet that you will see:

Amazon @amazon
Amazon Warehouse Deals: Deep discounts on used and open-box items amazon.com/gp/node/index....

Different businesses will get different results from Twitter. Because of the real-time, continuously scrolling stream of tweets, people need to be monitoring Twitter regularly to see your posts. Those who use Twitter frequently often do this from the smart phone, which makes it work best for location based tweets and instant deals, such as what you might get from a nearby restaurant.

You can of course tweet about anything you want. I tend to tweet about eCommerce. If you'd like to follow me on Twitter, here is my page:

https://Twitter.com/WebStoresLtd

Google+

This is Google's answer to Facebook. It deserves its own book (which Guy Kawasaki has already written called "What the Plus!"). Besides the fact that this platform is owned by Google (which helps with search engine rankings), here are some reasons why Google+ is important to your business:

- 100,000 character post size limit (compared to 63,206 characters on Facebook and 140 characters on Twitter).
- Video conferencing with ten people (known as Google Hangouts)
- Your posts can be seen by any follower as well as the general public
- After-the-fact editing of posts
- Grouping posts with comments and responses
- Automatic display of photos in posts
- Display photo albums in posts

The point is, Google+ has powerful and sophisticated features that other social media sites don't have. As more and more people jump on the Google+ bandwagon, it is important that your company have a presence there as well. But remember, like everything on the Internet, just having a presence isn't enough—you have to work it in order to get results.

Here is the link to Amazon's Google Plus page:

https://plus.google.com/+Amazon/

Here is the link to the WebStores Ltd Google Plus page: https://plus.google.com/+Webstoresltd1

Pinterest

Often regarded as a place where women hang out and share ideas, there is a lot that Pinterest can be used for. Pinterest is a great way to get others to market for you! The reason is, most "pins" are actually "re-pins". People spend more time on Pinterest than any other social network and it is the third largest source of referral traffic on the Internet. Conversion rates from Pinterest traffic are 50% higher than Facebook and they spend 2.5 times as much.

Pinterest boards are searchable by Google, so you want to make sure you properly tag all of your pins with appropriate keywords in the summary. I recommend creating graphics for your pins that are 554 pixels wide and 3 times longer than they are wide—these stand out better than horizontal images. You should also use a background color other than white to make the pin stand out. Be sure to include text on your images. Within the description of the pin, add a hashtag with your company name, such as #WebStoresLtd. That way, when someone re-pins your pin, your name will still be associated with the pin and you will be found more easily.

When browsing products on a brand website, sharing that product via social media buttons is a great way to express interest in that product, announce plans to buy it, or spread your liking for a product after buying it. A recent study done by 8th Bridge, after analyzing 872 retailers, concluded that Pinterest's 'Pin It' button has now overtaken Facebook's 'Like' button and Twitter's 'Tweet' button on brands' product pages. According to 8th Bridge, 62% of brands have Pin It buttons, 61% have Tweet buttons,

59% have Like buttons, and 42% have Google+1 buttons. While these percentages may be close, the values of each of these social media shares is not likely equal. What are social media shares really worth? In an article on Bloomberg BusinessWeek, according to social media backup provider Backupify, roughly estimated values are as follows:

- a Foursquare check-in is worth 40¢
- a LinkedIn search is worth 12.4¢
- a Facebook "share" is 2.4¢
- a Yelp review is worth $9.13
- a Tweet is worth 1/10th of a cent.
- a Pin generates 78 cents in sales

This information led blogger Zoe Waldron to the conclusion that a "Pin" is more valuable than a "Like" or a "Tweet". It does clearly show that providing social sharing buttons on your site can be good for business.

Amazon does not appear to have its own presence on Pinterest, but there are a lot of people that "pin" products from Amazon, giving them great exposure. One way you can use Pinterest is to add a "Pin it" button to your website, so others can spread the word about your products. Here is the link for doing this:

http://business.pinterest.com/widget-builder/#do_pin_it_button

Follow this link to see various boards and pins that others have created on Amazon's behalf:

http://www.pinterest.com/search/boards/?q=Amazon.com

Here is where you can follow me on Pinterest:
http://www.pinterest.com/gregjameson/

LinkedIn

LinkedIn is a business network. LinkedIn generates more B2B leads than any other social network. If you are looking to conduct business deals, whether they be consulting gigs or trying to find a joint venture partner, LinkedIn is the social network in which you want to participate.

Like both Facebook and Google, LinkedIn has given us some great tools to work with, then has taken them away. This should be fair warning—you cannot rely on having your Internet presence be tied to a site that is outside of your control. One of the great features that is now missing is question and answers.

LinkedIn has a job search feature that allows you to find not only traditional jobs, but consulting gigs. Unlike Facebook, LinkedIn does not have an overall news feed where you can see the latest from everyone. But the real power of LinkedIn comes with its groups. You can sign up for as many as fifty groups. And each group does have its own news feed. More importantly, groups are where you can interact with others and make connections. If you are going to take advantage of LinkedIn, make sure you are active in groups.

The groups you choose should be ones where your customers hang out, not your competitors. For example, if you are a real estate agent, don't just hang out in real estate groups, but get involved in community groups, school groups, etc.

A great tool that LinkedIn provides is the ability to export your contact list so you can email them. This can be a great way to build your email list, but your LinkedIn contacts are not the same as your subscribers, so be sure you don't spam them. Just because they are connected to you on LinkedIn does not mean that they have subscribed to your emails.

Most likely, you will also want to create a company LinkedIn page, not just a personal profile. Here is the link to the Amazon LinkedIn page:

www.linkedin.com/company/Amazon

And here is the link to the WebStores Ltd LinkedIn page:

http://www.linkedin.com/company/webstores-ltd

Location—Based Sites

Foursquare, Yelp, TripAdvsior, etc.—You don't need to do much with these sites, but you should be registered with them and set up a profile. Others like to check-in on Foursquare, which allows them to market for you. Anytime you can make it easy for others to check-in at your location or write a review about your products and services, you should do this! The same goes for Yelp—make it easy for people to write reviews about your company. If you are a local company, the comments posted by others on these kinds of sites can make a big impact on your business. In fact, as we saw in the discussion on Pinterest, a Yelp review can be worth a lot of money to your business, so you should encourage your customers to post these on your behalf. You can create your own business listing on Yelp.com (and I encourage you do to this). Once a Yelp listing has been created, either by you or a customer, be sure to claim the listing so you can manage it. That way you can respond to reviews that are posted on Yelp.

Affiliate Marketing

Affiliate marketing is a type of performance based marketing where retailers reward influencers for each new customer acquired through the influencer's own marketing efforts. The expression 'affiliate marketing' has traditionally been used in an online context, but arguably, the concept existed way before the World Wide Web. For example, if you referred someone to a store and they gave you a discount the next time you came in, that's affiliate marketing. (i.e., tell them Greg sent you). Of course the Internet revolutionized everything.

William J. Tobin conceived, implemented, and patented affiliate marketing as we know it. He set-up the first affiliate program for his company, PC Flowers & Gifts in 1989. In 1994 a company named CDnow launched an affiliate program that allowed websites to review albums and get paid a referral fee. However, it was Amazon who really put affiliate marketing on the map with the launch of its affiliate program in 1996. This is considered a key milestone in affiliate marketing as it attracted widespread global interest.

The story goes that a lady asked Amazon if she could sell dog books on her website. Her dog website was clearly a niche that Amazon wasn't targeting directly, so they agreed to pay her a commission on each sale her website brought to Amazon. The rest as they say is history. Today, over 40% of Amazon's sales still come from affiliate referrals.

That's significant, especially because tax law changes have made affiliate programs less attractive for out-of-state-referrals. In fact, if you live in Colorado like I do (as well as California, New York, Minnesota, Illinois and others), you can no longer be an Amazon affiliate because state tax laws require Amazon to treat their affiliates as if they have a physical location in that state and thus collect sales tax. As a result, Amazon has shut down its affiliate program if you live in a state that has enacted a so-called "Amazon" type affiliate nexus law.

While Amazon offers a myriad of features so that you can create different kinds of links to specific products on their site and then get paid for it when one of your customers purchases something from Amazon, the true power of affiliate links come from making your links appear to be a referral. For example, I have a customer who blogs about hunting and fishing. His readers visit his website to see what he has to say about hunting or fishing, or perhaps a new recipe he heard about for preparing game. When he writes his Blog, if he recommends a specific product and links to that product from Bass Pro Shops, his readers might purchase it. Of course, if he's smart (and he is), the link includes his affiliate id so he gets paid for the sale.

Lots of people have made money by becoming affiliates and selling other people's products, especially when using the referral link method I just mentioned, or blogging about a product and hiding the link in the content of the writing. ***But the real money with affiliate marketing comes from copying Amazon and being the one who pays out the commissions on affiliate sales.***

Today, anyone can run their own affiliate program. And the good thing is, you don't pay for clicks, you pay for sales. So if you have a local gardening club that links to your site, and this link results in a sale, then you pay them an agreed upon percentage of the sale. You keep track of this by including a code or ID in the domain name, so you know exactly where your traffic came from. Affiliate tracking software may be built into your shopping cart as an add-on, or you can contract this out to a third part service such as Commission Junction (CJ.com) or LinkShare. Of course, Google AdSense is essentially an affiliate program.

There are good reasons to use a third party company like Commission Junction—they handle all the logistics of running the program for you for a percentage of the sale. But you may have to meet certain requirements in order to work with them, and you may not want to give up another piece of the pie. If that is the case, then you can run your own affiliate program. If you have a WordPress website with an eCommerce plugin, <u>Affiliate Royale</u> is a great way for you to run your own affiliate program.

If you run your own program (like Amazon does), then you can hand-pick your affiliates. This gives you the ability to only work with companies who you want representing your products or services. I have another client who started out with a single affiliate. My client makes all-natural protein bars. He had a single affiliate who happened to be a blogger about health and nutrition. This blogger had a significant following. As an affiliate partner, she blogged about what a great product my client had, and provided an affiliate link to his website. Then she also sent out an email with her affiliate link in it. (As mentioned in the email section of this book, these kind of affiliate referrals are a great way to grow your list). The result of a single affiliate was that they went from very few sales to turning this into a real business almost overnight.

Press Releases

Press releases are a great way to get other people to market for you, as Amazon has clearly figured out. Amazon got a huge boost in its early day when Oprah Winfrey interviewed Jeff Bezos. Getting that kind of exposure may not happen all the time, but it can be increased by sending out press releases.

Right before Christmas last year Amazon cleverly staged two press releases. The first was about Sunday delivery. Amazon is large enough that they struck a deal with the US Post Office to deliver packages on Sunday for the Amazon Prime customers (more about

Prime later when I discuss membership sites). So someone could place an order on Friday night and have it delivered before they went to work on Monday.

The second press release one-upped themselves when they talked about 30 minute delivery in selected markets using drones to send a package from an Amazon warehouse directly to your door right after you placed the order. This ended up being carried by all the major news channels including a "60 Minutes interview" right before Cyber Monday as well as having everyone on the Internet talk about it. The technology isn't ready yet, they don't have approval from the FAA to fly thousands of private drones around our skies, and they haven't figured out how to prevent theft, but it got a huge buzz about Amazon right before the Christmas ordering season. Brilliant!

I remember sending out paper press releases weeks in advance with my first company. This resulted in landing a number of magazine articles, even several cover stories, and huge lines waiting to see us at various tradeshows. The concept still works today, but the time frame is significantly shorter (although faxed press releases are still valid). Online news sources, magazines,

Blog writers, radio and TV shows are all looking for exciting content that they can report on. You can supply this to them in the form of a press release and let them do the marketing for you, just like Amazon.

Press releases are not known to help with SEO, so you have to target where and to whom you send your press release. So, the question is, once you write a press release, who do you send it to so that it will get picked up? There are several places, some of which charge you for distribution, and others are free. Here are a few:

Free Press Release Sites:

PR.com—Not only will they distribute your press releases, but you can also set up a full company profile. **I recommend this one.**

PRBuzz.com—Completely free distribution to search engines, news sites, and blogs.

PRLog.org—Free distribution to Google News and other search engines.

The top press release distribution sites will allow you to include links, tagging and branding as part of their free or paid packages.

However, they all place various limitations on their free services.

Depending on your needs, however, the free services might be more than sufficient.

Your local newspaper—Definitely submit your releases to your local newspaper (and/or TV news outlet if you live in a bigger market).

Paid Press Release Sites

PRWeb
PRNewswire

Before you send out your press release, I recommend setting up a Google Alert. Google Alerts are email updates of the latest relevant Google results (web, news, etc.) based on your queries. That way, when your press release goes out, you will be able to monitor if anyone is mentioning you.

Create your alerts at: http://www.google.com/alerts

O—OFFER SOMETHING
FOR FREE

If you do build a great experience, customers tell each other about that. Word of mouth is very powerful.

—Jeff Bezos

OK, I've spent a lot of time talking about getting plenty of traffic to your site. Now that they are there, what is your objective? *It shouldn't be to make a sale the first time they visit your site, it should be to have them give you their name and contact information.* Amazon spent their first five years without showing a profit because they were more interested in building their market than in making a quick sale.

But the question arises as to why someone should give you their information—what's in it for them? Why would someone provide you with their name, email address, and phone number (after all, you might call them or send them a bunch of emails!).

The answer of course is that you should give them something of value in order to entice them to give you this information. This is often called "link bait". And it has to be significant—a coupon for 10% off will probably not get you many names.

But the most amazing thing about giving away something of value is the word of mouth it generates—truly getting others to market for you.

Cyberbase Trading Post

My first experience with the power of free came as the result of an experiment. I was a Scoutmaster and needed to create some certificates for some of my scouts who had just gone through the troop-level junior leadership training program to show that they had completed this course. Since I knew how to program in ColdFusion, and a new tag had come out that allowed you to generate PDF files on the fly from content that you supplied, I decided to put together a quick little program where I could enter in the name of each scout and have the program generate the certificate for me.

This little program ended up doing what I needed it to do, so I decided to share it with a few of my adult friends who were also involved in scouting. I emailed about 20 people and sent them a link to my certificate program asking them what they thought about this and to let me know if they found it useful. Within 24 hours I started receiving emails from all over the world thanking me for putting this program together and giving me unsolicited testimonials like:

> *I love this program. I will enjoy using it for different awards not only for Scouting, but for recognizing area businesses. Thank You.*

LOVE THIS SITE! THANK YOU!

Thank you for this boon. I am promoting it heavily at my Roundtable.

I have forwarded this website to many other Scouters.

Incredible website. I recommend it to everyone in Scouts.

Very cool idea, I am sending the web address to my council's Sr. District Exec to be passed on to all other units in the council.

*This site was recommended by other leaders and I viewed the certificates they made an*d was very impressed. Thank you.

I appeared to be on to something and didn't even know it. In the Internet world, this is known as viral marketing. Essentially it is a digital form of Word of Mouth. You need to create something that people want to share with others.

I quickly modified the program to allow users more flexibility. The steps involved in creating a certificate involved:

- Choosing between a vertical (portrait) or horizontal (landscape) orientation.
- Selecting one of about 70 background styles
- Picking the style of "seal" you wanted to use, a ribbon color, and the placement of the seal.
- Entering the text, fonts, and sizes you desired for each text box.

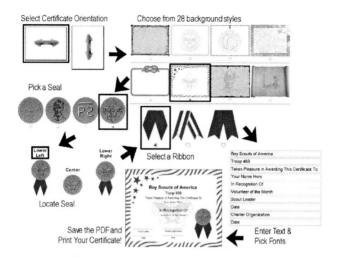

From this information, the program would generate a custom PDF that you could then print on your own printer. However, before the certificate was displayed as a PDF file, a small message would appear that said *"Hey! Cool Certificate. In order to print your certificate, please provide us with your email so we can send you a link."* The user would then have to enter their email before printing their certificate. Since the work of creating the certificate had already been done, most people were happy to enter their email—I did receive a few bogus emails, but I'd present the certificate anyways—the link was just emailed to them as a backup.

Anyways, I began getting as many as 30 to 40 emai addresses every day. I thought I might get in trouble with the Boy Scouts for creating this program, but instead, they featured me on their official Blog with a link to my website! I began getting people from the national scout office using the program as well.

I modified the final screen again, saying "If you enjoyed using this program, please consider making a small donation to help me keep this site open and free of charge". Then I put in a PayPal donate button—and I started getting donations—sometimes for as much as $50. You read that right—fifty, not five. Clearly you could buy a nice plaque for less than that, much less creating a certificate on your own. I later designed some custom –made certificate frames and allowed the user to order a frame for their certificate if they wanted to. I have never charged for this program—donations and purchases are totally optional. Five years later I continue to have people use this program every single day from countries all over the world. Giving something away for free can be big.

But the thing is, you have to give away something that is valuable enough that your visitors will willingly provide you with their emai addresses so that you can continue to market to them. I now have thousands of email addresses of scouters. But if I had simply put an input box on my website that said "join my mailing list" or "sign up for my newsletter", how many emails do you think I would have gotten? Very few.

Case Studies

Vista Print

Vista Print gives away free business cards. The cards are of good quality and you only pay shipping. Unlike many free offers, the shipping is reasonable—they aren't trying to pay for the cost of the cards by raising shipping fees. Instead they are trying to recover the cost of the free business cards by printing a small promotion on the back of the cards with their website address—helping to spread the word about their company. Not only do they get exposure this way, but people love to talk about how they got their business cards for free.

Of course you can update to a premium card for a reasonable fee, which removes the VistaPrint branding from the back of the card. And you can order all sorts of other business-branding items from them including brochures, postcards, letterhead, etc.—all of which they try to upsell you on during checkout (more about that under "Request an Action".)

Elizabeth Country Corner

Can't think of what to give away for free that offers enough value? Try using the power of others—and let them give away something for free on your behalf! That's what Elizabeth Country Corner does once a year with its annual animal swap. As a feed store, they host an animal swap in their parking lot where people from all over the area can come and unload their unwanted pets—cats, dogs, rabbits, and even horses. And people come to claim their "free" pet. Not only is this great publicity for the feed store, but the ingenious thing about this is that after someone picks up their free bunny or cat, then they go inside the store to buy food, shavings, cages, and toys for their new pet!

Skype

When people think 'Skype', they usually think 'free calls'. That's because Skype-to-Skype voice calls, video calls and group calls on your computer are absolutely free. So how does Skype leverage this to make money? They have upgraded or premium services including Skype to land-line calls, monthly subscriptions, and group video. But their basic free service is enticing enough that 31 million people have signed up and end spending an average of $96 year per user.

So what can you give away that will entice people to give you their email addresses so you can market to them?

Perhaps you sell fabric—how about providing a free pattern they can download? Or maybe you sell woodworking tools and could provide free plans for building a rocking chair? How about a free (downloadable) movie about your niche? Notice none of these actually cost you any money, because they are downloadable digital files. You could certainly offer free physical goods, but that would cost you money both for the product and the shipping. Think creatively! Look back at the example of the YMCA in the Facebook section of this book. Often people end up offering a "white-paper" or eBook. Those items are over-used. Try to come up with something relevant to what you do that truly adds value to someone and you'll be pleasantly surprised at the results.

What about a drawing for a larger ticket item? People would love to get a TV, digital camera, or even tickets to the super bowl. You probably can't afford to give away an iPad for every email address you collect, but if the prize is large enough and the odds are good enough, people may give you their email for a chance to win something of value.

Get them to fill out an application!

One of the biggest mistakes retailers make on their websites is thinking that someone is going to buy from them on their first visit. This would be like getting married on your first date. You are far better off getting their email address when they visit so that you can follow up with them later.

If 1% of your visitors buy on their first visit, but 10% are willing to give you their email because of something you are giving away, you just increased your chance for a sale by 10 times! That is why I recommend simply trying to sell a first time visitor on filling out an application rather than on making a purchase. If you are a wholesaler that sells to retail establishments, your goal should be to get them to fill out an application to become one of your approved resellers.

Yet almost every B2B (business to business) website I see, act just like most consumer sites, trying to sell products. What they should be doing is trying to sell themselves and why someone would want to retail their products. This is the old radio station acronym: WIFM (What's in it for me?). Even though Amazon is a retail site, the ideal wholesale site would behave like Amazon, with a homepage that changed for a first time visitor to something more relevant for a returning buyer.

Of course, offering something for free to the first time visitor as a way to get them to fill out your dealer application is still valid, even for B2B purchasers. Perhaps your home page for these visitors would include an offer for a free sample product upon approval of their application to become a reseller of your products.

In my previous book, "Grow Your Online Sales", I discussed how the policy pages on your website should talk about why someone *should* do business with you, rather than (like most policy statements), why they shouldn't. The same applies to your dealer application—make sure that both the copy on the page and the application itself are selling the prospective dealer on why they should be doing business with you.

Example:

This is a real wholesale application form that is typical to many websites.

In order to buy at wholesale you must meet the following minimum guidelines…

1) *you must buy the minimum of $XXX per order in order to buy wholesale*

2) *you must be buying the product for resale (federal tax-id AND sales tax number required) not for own use but to sell to others*

3) *you must provide ONE of the following…*
   A) *your tax id number*
   B) *articles of incorporation*
4) *you must provide ONE of the following…*
   A) *a photo of your retail establishment (a store front photo and inside your store)*
   B) *a copy of your published catalogue or brochure*
   C) *a URL location of your active eCommerce website*
5) *you must provide, in your first year, proof that you are promoting our line of products.*
6) *In order to retain your wholesale account you must do the following.*
   A) *in your first calendar year buy at wholesale at least $XXX*
   B) *in your second calendar year and thereafter buy at wholesale at least $XXX*
7) *you must pay your invoices in a timely manner. Most lower volume resellers must pay for goods in advance by credit card or other payment.*
8) *understand and agree to the shipping policy.*

What if you re-worded this to show the prospective buyer that by working with you, they stand to make a lot of money?:

Our resellers form the core of our business and we are excited that you would like to represent our products! To protect our resellers, we have certain guidelines that allow you to purchase from us at wholesale including:

1) *minimum orders of $XXX per order insure that not just anyone can buy at wholesale.*

2) *federal tax-id and sales tax number so that you can resell the product at margins that increase your profits.*

3) *Please provide ONE of the following so we can verify you as one of our partners...*

   A) *a photo of your retail establishment (a store front photo and inside your store)*

   B) *a copy of your published catalogue or brochure*

   C) *a URL location of your active eCommerce website*

4) *When you buy at least $XXX worth of wholesale product in the first year, this indicates that we are helping you be successful and that it makes sense for both of us to continue our relationship with an active account.*

5) *Once we have an established relationship, we welcome the opportunity to discuss payment terms other than credit cards.*

6.) *As consideration for you taking the time to fill out our reseller application, we would like to send you a sample product from our catalog at no cost so you can evaluate the quality of our offerings.*

Which of these do you think is more likely to influence a prospective company to do business with you?

W—WIN THEIR TRUST

The best customer service is if the customer doesn't need to call you, doesn't need to talk to you. It just works... Your brand is formed primarily, not by what your company says about itself, but what the company does... Your brand is what people say about you when you're not in the room.

—Jeff Bezos

Ratings & Reviews

Customers trust each other more than they do marketers. Study after study reinforces the fact that customers trust each other's opinions more than they do any messages that emanate directly from marketers themselves. Online customer ratings and reviews influence more customers to buy than any other form of online advertising. Adding online reviews to your website has proven to:

- Increase conversion
- Increase average transaction amount
- Improve customer satisfaction
- Lower product return rates

In fact, 62% of shoppers read consumer-written product reviews online, 80% say their purchase decisions have been directly influenced by reviews, and 70% of shoppers share product reviews with their friends, family or colleagues.

This is Amazon's Dirty Little Secret: They let others do the selling for them. Customers write product reviews and create significant amounts of high quality content regarding the products for sale on Amazon. Additionally, they rank the products with a rating of 1 to 5 stars, and these rankings are averaged so other consumers can see how people feel about a product. Both positive and negative reviews are posted, so Amazon is truly winning the consumer's trust. In fact, it has been estimated that 55% of people visit Amazon prior to purchasing anything on the Internet, specifically because of their product reviews—this is true even if they don't end up purchasing from Amazon.

For years eBay provided a similar ranking for sellers—allowing buyers to see how a seller would take care of them if they were to make a purchase. Again, it's all about winning trust and reviews go a long way towards building trust with a potential customer. This is the primary reason why Amazon outsells all other online stores, and why you should emulate them.

But there are some problems with online reviews: Fake reviews and relevancy.

It might be possible for someone to post fake reviews, thus causing your customers to lose trust, so you do have to keep an eye out for this.

If you only display 10 reviews on a page, and there are more than 10 reviews, then earlier reviews might be hidden from a customer. This was a problem that Amazon faced because popular products would get many reviews. Being able to sort reviews based on rating helps, but Amazon found this wasn't enough. Because of a very subtle yet clever feature, Amazon makes the best of both the positive and negative reviews easy to find. And that feature, per Jarod Spool, is responsible for more than $2,700,000,000 of new revenue for Amazon every year. Not bad for what is essentially a simple question: "Was this review helpful to you?"

Amazon needed a way to editorialize reviews, without paying their staff to sit down and figure out which reviews were best. Once again, they used other people to do this for them by asking the question, "Was this review helpful to you?" Customers could then vote for reviews, whether positive or negative, and those reviews that customers found most helpful would rise to the top. Genius!

Robin Daniels of Salesforce.com, says that by delighting your customers, you can turn them into effective sales people who persuade friends, family and colleagues to use your products and services. "Sales people are good but there's nothing that beats a recommendation from an independent source," Daniels concludes. "It is very powerful to have your customers selling for you and it offers more credibility than any sales person."

Amazon has earned a reputation for strong service by letting customers get what they want without ever talking to an employee. An example was provided by Bloomberg BusinessWeek, where they told how Lisa Dias purchased a book on Amazon that was advertised as "like new". The seller wasn't Amazon itself, but one of the merchants that market through its website. Still, Dias went ahead and dished out $24.95 for the paperback.

When the book arrived at her New Jersey home, though, it wasn't anywhere close to new. The worksheets were already filled in with someone else's scrawlings. She felt burned but didn't do anything about it until November. She first tried the merchant and didn't get any response. Then Dias called Amazon. The company immediately gave her a refund, without her having to return the book. She's still a bit baffled that Amazon paid her money the company never received in the first place. "I felt like they stood up for me," says Dias.

Then there's the story from George Parker, who bought one of the first Amazon Kindles. After enjoying it for a week; he dropped it on the floor and stood on it. He called Amazon and explained what had happened. They said they would ship him a new Kindle that day and that he should return the old one in their pre-paid package. George asked how much this would cost. Nothing, they said—and he became a customer for life.

Or the story of Henry Blodget who rented the movie Casablanca from Amazon. When you rent a movie from Amazon, you have to use their "player" which streams the video. Says Blodget:

> *"Like a lot of streaming video players, it often seized up, forcing me to start again. That was annoying. But it wasn't unexpected. And I had no idea (and still don't) whether the problem was on Amazon's end or due to my Internet connection.*
>
> *Having problems with streaming video, especially streaming HD video, is obviously nothing new. The technology is still klugy enough that there are problems as often as there aren't problems. And I have long since gotten used to them. But, in the end, Amazon's streaming service delivered a beautiful HD experience, and I got my story.*

So imagine my surprise this morning when I got the email below from Amazon."

> Hello,
> We noticed that you experienced poor video playback while watching the following rental(s) on Amazon Video On Demand:
> Casablanca
> We're sorry for the inconvenience and have issued you a refund for the following amount(s):
> $2.99
> …We hope to see you again soon.
> Amazon Video On Demand Team

"Amazon "noticed that I experienced poor video playback…"
They did? And they decided to give me a refund because of that? Wow."

Or consider this story: If you order a PlayStation online and it gets snatched from your doorstep instead of being delivered safely to your living room, that's your problem, right? Or maybe it's the delivery service's problem. Or it's the problem of the neighbor who signed for your expensive gaming system but didn't bother to bring it inside to protect it from sticky fingers. Wherever the blame lands, it's definitely not the problem of the company who fulfilled their end of the bargain by shipping the system using a secure method. However, when this scenario happened to an Amazon customer a few years ago, he called them to beg—plead—to see if there was anything that could be done because his son was expecting a PlayStation from Santa. Much to the customer's shock, they not only sent another, but they didn't even charge him for shipping. It even made it there on time for Christmas.

It's that kind of customer service that has made Amazon a legend and propelled them into the same circle as Apple and Nordstrom's.

It's interesting that Amazon's current logo was designed to depict a smile that goes from A to Z. "This signifies that the company is willing to deliver everything to everyone, anywhere in the world."

Amazon.com employees spend two days every two years working at the customer service desk, even the CEO. This practice is to help all workers understand the customer service process.

Jeff Bezos says, "Internally, customer service is a component of customer experience. Customer experience includes having the lowest price, having the fastest delivery, having it reliable enough so that you don't need to contact [anyone]. Then you save customer service for those truly unusual situations."

Testimonials

In addition to product reviews, you should display customer testimonials. My recommendation is that you scatter testimonials throughout your website so that they appear on every single page, not just a page called "testimonials (that people may never visit).

Most people like to share their opinions if you ask them. Every time you ask a customer to provide feedback on a purchase, it makes them feel important and valued—like they weren't just another transaction. It demonstrates to them that you really care about what they think and you want to keep them happy. Customers also like feeling that they're involved and contributing to the process of making your business better. The number one reason most businesses don't get reviews and referrals isn't because they aren't good at what they do or customers are too busy to provide them. It's because many businesses simply don't ask for reviews or make it easy for customers to do it.

1) **Ask for them.** It sounds ridiculously simple, but if you don't ask for reviews, you probably won't get them. Businesses have to get in the habit of asking for customer reviews as close to the point of customer satisfaction as possible. That point is usually right after the purchase or once they've had a chance to try out their purchase. If you don't ask, they'll assume you're not interested. Few customers—happy or not—will provide feedback unless invited to do so.

2) **Make it easy.** Don't believe for a minute that a customer doesn't like the opportunity to provide feedback. Most people will take at least two seconds to click on a simple star rating system. If they really are too busy, they will politely decline or ignore the comment card. But the easier you can make it for customers to review their experience with you, the more feedback you will receive. If they bought it online, they'll probably be interested in reviewing it online. Also, provide the opportunity to offer anonymous feedback for those who are hesitant to give their name.

3) **Create an online survey.** There are a number of online survey companies such as SurveyMonkey.com that can make it very easy to gather feedback via Web-based surveys. Many are easy-to-use, fast, efficient and an inexpensive way to gather data from customers. If your business has a Facebook page, you can even create a survey for free using the Questions tool.

4) **Offer incentives.** Encourage customers to provide reviews by offering an incentive such as a chance to win something of value. The idea is to motivate customers to take the time to provide feedback, not bribe them. Companies that offer discounts or give freebies for reviews can taint their results because it looks like they're trying to buy only positive feedback.

5) **Include a link on receipts.** Have you noticed how long receipts are these days? That's typically because at the bottom, companies are inviting customers to participate in online surveys regarding their shopping experience through a website or a toll-free phone number. It's a great place to ask for reviews because a customer may toss the bag or the packaging, but they're likely to hang on to the receipt. This is true even if they made the purchase online.

6) **Include a comment card with every purchase.** Whether you put it in the bag with a purchase or slip it into a shipping order, a comment card with either a website or prepaid postage has a good chance of being filled out and returned.

7) **Add reviews to your website.** Just like Amazon®, add a simple star rating system to your products on your website with a note requesting "Give us your review" or "Be the first to review this product." Be sure to also leave space

for customers to type their comments. You could learn a lot about your customers' favorite features or product flaws quickly. WordPress site can use a plugin like Mage Reviews to accomplish this. WebStores Ltd wholesale sites have this feature built-in.

8) **Follow up emails.** Once the customer has had a chance to use their purchase, follow up with an email asking for a product review or comments. If they are particularly happy, you're likely to hear about it. However, sending the email too soon or too late can affect your responses.

9) **Follow up phone calls.** A bit more old-fashioned is the follow up phone call to make sure a customer's experience was up to par—yet, for some, it does offer a more personal touch than email.

10) **Follow up postcard.** More costly than email because of postage, follow up postcards are still a good way to solicit feedback—especially with older customers.

11) **Provide in-store access.** This includes in-store signage asking for feedback and the classic customer comment box on the counter by the register. For a more modern take on it, set up a computer nearby so customers can enter their ratings and provide feedback that you can track easily.

12) **Bring in outside help.** If you have the time and resources, bring in a professional research company to help you design a thorough survey. Customers will often be more honest with a third party than they will be with the company directly. Best of all, the research company can provide an objective perspective and help you interpret the data collected to see where the greatest opportunities for improvement lie.

How and when to ask for testimonials

The best time to ask for a testimonial is when a client tells you about a result you helped him or her achieve. You can use this as a springboard to ask them to write you a formal testimonial. Another optimal time to ask is when you have finished your work with a client, or when a program is complete. But you typically have to ask.

HOW you ask for a testimonial is every bit as important as asking for one. Consider this:

> *"I need to get some testimonials for my website. Would you consider writing something for me?"*

Versus this:

> *"I love that you made that happen, George! Would you be willing to let me feature you on my website as a client success story so that other people can be inspired by you?"*

Position the testimonial as something of service (because it is!) and something that will promote them. (Because it will!)

Make sure you ask for THEIR story and THEIR results. You do not want a testimonial telling the world how great YOU are.

Tell your client exactly what you want in your testimonial. Here's a formula:

1. Share where you were before.
2. Share some tangible results you got.
3. Share where you are now.

Some specific questions you might ask include:

- What was the obstacle that would have prevented you from buying this product?
- What did you find as a result of buying this product?
- What specific feature did you like most about this product?
- What would be three other benefits about this product?
- Would you recommend this product? If so, why?
- Is there anything you'd like to add?

If your client is daunted by writing (as many people are), ask them to just jot down a few bullet points. You can help edit and let them give the final approval.

Have you ever seen a glowing testimonial followed only by a set of initials and a city?

Kind of wrecks the whole vibe, doesn't it? That's because it seems fake! We don't know who "T.K., Colorado Springs, CO" is.

But "Terri Knight, Colorado Springs, CO" is a real person with a real smile. Do not ignore the impact of this.

Always include a photo, full name and (if applicable) website address or business name. This provides valuable exposure for your client—and also lends credibility to the testimonial.

Your clients are the reason your business exists. So please don't forget to thank them for taking the time to help you build your business. Consider sending a handwritten thank you note or even a small token of appreciation. This is perfectly acceptable and is not a bribe if you do this after the fact.

Of course trust can be established in other ways as well. Using SSL (Secure Socket Layer) technology during checkout is a must. Providing high quality photos and description can help build trust. Add press mentions is a good idea. Put a face to your brand, and engage people via social media. And don't hide—if you have a physical location, put a map of where you are. Add your phone number to the header or footer of your site so it is easy to find on every single page of your site. Make your "terms and conditions" page show why someone should do business with you, not why they shouldn't. Use third party credibility seals. Have a clear and concise return policy. Everything about your website should be geared at winning the customers trust.

If you are a wholesaler and you allow anyone and everyone to see your prices and order from you, this can erode the trust of your dealers. Part of winning a reseller's trust is deciding who you are going to sell to. In the retail world, most shops will sell to anyone who places an order. Some wholesalers will do this as well, providing the volume is high enough. However, if you sell your products to every shop, you might lose credibility with all the shop owners. This could cause less demand for your products. If you limit your sales geographically and/or by type of store, you can provide an incentive to shop owners as they would have an exclusive. So you may want to limit who you sell to.

Wholesale distributors must build deep relationships with customers based on an understanding of the true value created by their services and activities. This is a major difference between wholesale and retail. Retail sales are concerned with word of mouth, but wholesale sales require an on-going relationship. When done right, doing this online can actually help you strengthen this relationship; if done poorly it can cost you.

Recommended WordPress Plugins:

For star ratings and reviews:

- Mage Reviews (http://wordpress.org/plugins/mage-reviews/) or
- CD Star Rating (http://www.gdstarrating.com/)

For displaying random testimonials:

- Perfect Quotes (http://perfectspace.com/perfect-quotes-a-wordpress-plugin/)

E—ENGAGING EXPERIENCE

We see our customers as invited guests to a party, and we are the hosts. It's our job every day to make every important aspect of the customer experience a little bit better... The number one rule has to be: Don't be boring.

—Jeff Bezos

What kind of experience do customers have when they visit your site? The first page should be about what the reader is looking for—not about you! Let them know what the site will do for them. All too often I see websites where all the site does is talk about how great the company is, and never provides any information that is beneficial to the user. That is not the case with Amazon.

Amazon's homepage is never the same. With sections like 'New for you', 'More items to consider' and 'Recommendations for you in video games' Amazon is constantly tracking what you've browsed and what you've bought, then adjusting their messaging to you. The featured items when you visit Amazon are most certainly different than if I visit Amazon, because they are targeting products specifically to you.

Amazon is so confident of its ability to personalize the site for each user that the company hardly ever creates classic customer-segment personas, such as "soccer moms" or "gearheads." Such marketing standbys are too imprecise for Amazon. The site is personalized for every single customer. Amazon is the king of customer experience, so my advice is to emulate them.

Shopping on Amazon is easy. A really cool feature is that when you add an item to the cart, the cart is displayed (as one would expect), but additional products available for purchase are also displayed. Many online retailers like the idea of not displaying the cart, but instead sending the customer back to the product page so they can purchase more. The problem is, that isn't intuitive for the consumer, who then has to click on "cart" to see what is in there. And if they don't understand this system, they may inadvertently add the same item to the cart multiple times—which is a negative customer experience.

The alternative that most carts have adopted is to show the cart (like Amazon does), which is the logical thing to the buyer, but then have a button that says "Continue Shopping", because they assume that the customer won't understand that they can add other items to the cart without checking out, even though the navigation and search bar might be present. Amazon solves this neatly—they show the cart *and* they show additional products, all on the same page. Again, why not emulate this if it works so well?

Payment Solutions

If your order is under the $35 limit, Amazon suggests topping off your order to get free shipping. When you proceed to the checkout page, if you have ordered with Amazon before, you can check out with a single click. It is not necessary to re-enter any information unless something has changed. Most shopping cart software allows you to sign-in with a user name and password and your name and address is restored, but Amazon remembers you from previous visits, even without signing in. And they also store your credit card information—this is something that some consumers do not like (and they are given the option to turn off one-click checkout), and it is also something that as a small business owner, you may not be able to legally do. It's a great feature that for security reasons, your credit card company may not allow.

In order to save credit card information on an Internet server, your company would have to pass a series of strict PCI DSS (Payment Card Industry Data Security Standard) requirements. This is a time consuming and costly process. My recommendation for small businesses is that they use a hosted payment solution like PayPal, Evalon, ElementPS, or 2Checkout. Amazon also passes on this capability to small merchants with its Amazon Flexible Payment System, though many shopping carts don't integrate with it.

Using one of these hosted solutions, the payment solution is the company that must meet PCI requirements rather than the merchant. Essentially what happens is that the customer shops on your site, you collect all of their data except for their credit card information during checkout. The customer then select the Pay Now button, which transfers them to the hosted payment site where they enter their credit card information, and once the card has been approved, is returned to your site. The whole process is simple and in most cases un-obtrusive to the buying experience.

Product Descriptions

But with Amazon, the customer experience doesn't stop there. When you visit a product page, you will see that the descriptions of the product (at least the ones sold directly by Amazon and not a 3rd party selling on their site), contain lengthy and robust descriptions. You can usually find out everything you want about a product before purchasing it. There is not just a single image of the product—there are multiple views, and you can enlarge any of them to see the product in more detail.

It has been shown that 67% of consumers who have visited an online store with the intent of making a purchase left the site because the retailer did not provide enough information about the product in order for the consumer to feel comfortable enough to make the purchase online. That isn't the case with Amazon. People come to the Internet looking for information –so follow Amazon's lead and give it to them! As we saw in the information about SEO, Google also rewards sites with more content. Do not make the mistake of putting up only one product image with little or no information about it.

When it comes to the product descriptions, more is better. The length of copy should be longer than traditional ad copy. The Internet does not have a space limitation like traditional ads. Generally speaking, the longer the length of your copy, the more you are going to sell.

On the next page is a real example of a company that sells organic jams:

Compare this to one of my clients that also sells organic jams.

Which one are you more likely to buy from?

I was once asked by someone who sold pond equipment to look at his website. He said he was getting lots of traffic, but not many sales, but said his competitors were getting lots of sales. I asked to look at both his site and his competitor's site. Here is an example of what I saw on one of his pump pages:

I didn't see anything that would make me want to buy his pump. Next I looked at his competitor's site. As you can see, it included lots of information, including how much water the pump actually discharged:

I did another website review for a customer that sold leather purses. Like most people, they weren't complaining about not getting enough traffic to their website, but that they weren't getting enough sales. They asked me to look at their website, which included product descriptions that sounded like they came directly from the manufacturer. As the expert selling this product, they should have created their own descriptions. Here was a typical description on their site:

American West Purse #6530758 Carmel. Hand Tooled Leather. Guaranteed for life.

My recommendation wasn't that they just make a few changed, but instead to add multiple images of the purses, inside and out from all angles. Then create a whole new description that sounded appealed to the buyer's emotions and contained complete product detail such as:

The mere mentions of "AMERICAN WEST" conjures up images of cowboys and pathfinders in search of new frontiers. With this pioneering tradition, American West celebrates the human spirit that lives on in the hearts of many, still today, as in days gone by. It is this legacy that has inspired American West's products line, the leaders in Western handbags and accessories for more than 15 years. It is a legacy of quality, hand-crafted leather items made by hand—one at a time— that reflect the true values of the West.

American West stands behind their products with an unconditional manufacturer's guarantee by repairing or replacing the item, with no cost to the customer. All of their products carry a lifetime manufacturer's defect guarantee.

This vintage style collection blends basketweave and floral tooled designs on an aged mocha colored leather background. Leather whipstitching and antiques silver spots add decorative details to this traditional collection and are highlighted with a Western star concho and buckle set. Whether you buy this for yourself or give it as a gift…this American West Ladies Handbag will be something that is cherished for a lifetime.

This outstanding three compartment leather handbag is made of 100% hand-picked leather and features:

- *Inside middle zipper compartment*
- *Two open compartments on either side*
- *Flap over top snaps shut*
- *Inside pouches and zip compartment*
- *11" Shoulder Strap drop*
- *This is made from hand-tooled vegetable tanned antique brown leather*
- *Features a silver buckle with the Texas Lone Star Concho*
- *Measures 14" x 10" x 5"*

Each tooled piece is created by individual strikes… one by one…which creates more than just another leather handbag…a piece of art is created. All of their tooling patterns are created by individual craftsmen using mallets and small tooling dies to create their intricate artwork on leather.

Each tooled product is the culmination of thousands of individual die strikes. Unlike die pressed patterns, small inconsistencies and changes are proof of an artisan at work. Buckle sets, conchos and other silver hardware items are cast

in solid brass or zinc, the lavishly dipped in sterling silver.
Since silver had a natural tendency to varnish and scratch,
American West adds a protective layer of lacquer to each piece.

Obviously, crafting a description like this takes more effort and work, but remember, this is what sells!

The next example shows quite clearly how providing in depth information about your product can really help make the sale. This story is about a cowboy who lives in northern Wyoming. Each year he buys himself a new cowboy hat, and sells his old one on eBay. Now what do you think a used cowboy hat would sell for, especially one that is beat up and doesn't have much wear left in it? As it turns out, this enterprising fellow sells his used hat for considerably more than a new one! Rather than just saying "used cowboy hat for sale", he goes to great lengths to describe all of the adventures he's had while wearing that hat. If he fell off his horse into a river, he'll talk about that. If he saw a bear while wearing that hat, he'll describe that. He's not just selling a hat, he's selling an adventure.

This is key when selling products on the Internet. Customers can't see your product, other than through the pictures or videos you provide. They can't feel the product or ask you questions. It is your job to sell the product, and to do this, you must make your description do the selling for you.

Product Videos

To master the art of selling your products online, you first need to know the art of how to convince your potential clients to buy from you, and you need to know how to do this effectively.

A great way to be a virtual salesperson is to create a video about the product you are selling. You should create a video for every single product. If you look back to the section on YouTube, you will notice that I recommend uploading this product video to YouTube, tagging it with keywords about this specific product, and providing a link in the description back to the product page on your website. Then of course you need to embed this video on the product page. Today, people prefer to watch the Internet rather than read it. Imagine having a video associated with the products shown above: someone spreading jam on their favorite bread, the cowboy riding his horse as he talks about his hat, or viewing the pump in action.

Be sure to tell as much about your products as you can because it's likely that your potential customers will have little idea about them. Be as open as you can with your information, and the more you can give them, the easier their decision is to buy from you. Feed them the benefits, unique selling points, and features of your creations. Only by delivering such quality content like this, will they have good reason to take advantage of your products.

As a salesperson, you are responsible for getting information to your potential customer, and video is a great way to do this—use it!

> *"Traffic alone isn't enough. YOU are the expert; sell them on what you have to offer."*
>
> **—Greg Jameson**

Test Your Website

I can't stress enough how important it is to perform usability testing. I've seen numerous websites where the site owner knows how to navigate his or her own site, but their customers have no idea how to use it. In one case, when you clicked on the "Add to

Cart" button, it appeared that nothing had happened (in fact it had, but the cart wasn't displayed). As a result, users would click on the "Add to Cart" button multiple times, and never see how to view the cart and checkout.

If you want to know whether your website is easy enough to use, watch some people while they try to use it and note where they run into trouble. Then fix it, and test it again.

When should I test? Ideally, once per month. You should be running small usability tests continuously throughout the development process. The tests should be short and simple, so you can conduct them almost any time with little advance planning. Perhaps it is best not to view web design as a one-time project but as a continual work in progress.

How many users do I need? Three or four max. What kind of users? Grab some people. Anyone who can use a computer will do. The best-kept secret of usability testing is that it doesn't much matter who you test. It's a good idea to get representative users, but it's much more important to test early and often. Don't be embarrassed to ask friends and neighbors. Get people with different operating systems (Mac vs. PC) and different browsers (IE, Firefox, Safari, etc.).

How much time will it take? Thirty minutes to an hour per user. Keep it simple. Keep it small. Although it does take extra time to conduct usability tests, even simple ones, ultimately you will save time.

One of the nicest things about usability testing is that the results tend to be obvious to everyone who's watching. The serious problems are hard to miss.

In addition to the random human test described above, you may want to perform some automated testing as well. Why? Here is an example:

Firefox recently made some changes to their popular browser software. Many of our customers updated this software automatically, and then called us to complain that their website wasn't working. Neither of us had made any changes to their site, yet a problem had occurred. What this means is that simply because your site worked last week, doesn't mean it is functioning reliably today. There are many reasons why site problems can occur. For example:

- Automatic software updates that include email, databases, web server administration, and shopping cart functionality.
- Most likely you are on a shared server with many other websites. Changes in bandwidth used by these other sites or the addition of large new accounts on the same server could affect you.
- The data center where your site is hosted could experience problems from server changes or power outages.
- Browser changes can affect not only how your site appears, but as mentioned previously, how it functions.
- Links on your webpage to external sites can fail if the target site deletes the page or changes the URL. I even see our customers deleting or changing the names of their own pages, without also updating the links that point too them.
- Third party providers such as credit card processing services can make unannounced changes that can cause failures with essential pieces of your site.
- Security failures could cause your site to be hacked or attacked.

It is impossible to prevent these changes from occurring, and even if these changes are positive, they may create a temporary problem for your site. One method for insuring that you know when your site has stopped working is to use site monitoring services. Site monitoring takes place invisibly without you having to change anything on your site. Their software just goes to your site on a regular basis to perform a test. You select the pages to test and the alerts and reports you want to receive. Testing options include test frequency and the emergency procedures to follow when a problem is detected.

Testing your site on an hourly (or even daily) basis is not feasible except by using a software service. This is not a substitute for humans, who can test usability, but an additional form of testing to insure that the site is working. Site monitoring may just protect you from revenue loss, making it a cost effective insurance for your web business.

Mobile

With over 61 percent of the population now having a Smartphone, as part of testing your website, you want to be sure to test it on various mobile devices.

Amazon.com Inc. is the No. 1 mobile destination among mass merchants for U.S. smartphone owners accessing the mobile web and mobile apps, finds research giant Nielsen. In fact, a majority of smartphone owners who accessed the web or apps on their devices in 2013 shopped Amazon.com.

That is 76.1 million unique monthly visitors to Amazon's mobile website. On average, shoppers spent 38 minutes and one second on the m-commerce site or the Amazon app. One contributing factor to Amazon.com's success, mobile commerce experts say, is showrooming, which in this instance is when a consumer checks out a product in a bricks-and-mortar store but uses her smartphone to compare prices and possibly buy the product via mobile or later online. Fifty eight percent (58%) of adult smartphone owners regularly engage in showrooming, and the mobile resource most used by these shoppers is Amazon.com

Of course, if we are going to follow Amazon's lead here, you should consider creating your own mobile app, not just a mobile-friendly website. An app makes it easier for your customers to do business with you and that can be a big calling card. With 85% of users preferring an app over a mobile website, this may be a smart move for your business.

Here are some of the advantages of apps:

Ease of Use: It is very easy for users to navigate through and interact with mobile applications.

Cooler visuals: The graphics and effects on a mobile website can be very limited because of the bandwidth and technology. However, mobile apps have the capabilities to have superior graphics and effects, presenting a cooler looking visual to your users.

Usable Offline: Users do not have to be connected to a network or wireless connection to use mobile applications. Mobile websites always require the user to be connected to the Internet in some way while a lot of apps do not require Internet connection and can be used offline.

Speed: Mobile apps have the ability to run a lot faster than mobile websites.

Interactivity/Gaming: For interactive games (such as Words with Friends) an app is almost always going to be your best choice.

Easier to access data about users: Marketers are able to access a wide variety of data about mobile users such as demographics and geo-location through mobile apps.

Complex Calculations or Reporting: If you need something that will take data and allow you to manipulate it with complex calculations, charts or reports an app will help you do that very effectively.

Increase users' interaction time: When users have an app they like, they use it more frequently and for much longer amounts of time than the mobile website. Your app has to have enough value to get users to spend that much time interacting with your content.

Native Functionality or Processing: Mobile web browsers are getting increasingly good at accessing certain mobile-specific functions but if you need to access a user's camera or processing power, an app will do that much more effectively.

Shopping Cart Abandonment

Online retailers spend a lot of energy getting people to visit their sites, and once there, getting visitors to make a purchase. It can be discouraging then to view reports and see the number of people who have placed items in the cart, then don't complete the purchase. This is called cart abandonment, and it is a problem that faces most online stores. But is it really a problem?

How often does a customer begin their shopping experience online, primarily for price comparison, but then completes the sale at the physical store of the same merchant? This question is difficult to track. Frequently, however, someone will place items in the cart, and then complete the sale a few days later. I know I do this often—for example, I have a customer that needed some business cards. She wanted a price before ordering, so I went through the entire cart process, and then abandoned the cart, only to complete the sale a few days later after she had approved everything.

The average online shopper delays making a purchase by almost two days after initially visiting a retail site according to data from a leading Internet security company. After monitoring the shopping behavior of 163 million consumers completing 2.52 million transactions, McAfee SECURE discovered that the average customer waited 33 hours and 54 minutes, or nearly two days, between first visiting a retail site and making a purchase. In 64 percent of the cases, the shopper waited at least one day to buy.

This seemingly cautious behavior, which McAfee calls "digital window shopping," is really a somewhat normal shopping behavior wherein a potential customer loads items into a shopping cart and then leaves the retailer's site in search of more information, price comparison data, or even information about the merchant to ensure that the transaction and any customer service will be handled well.

What this suggests to me is that retailers should have a function to "save this cart", so the customer can log back in at a later time and complete the sale without having to start over. Amazon has this feature, but most online stores do not. Combined with an email reminder that they still have not completed the checkout process, this could be a major enhancement to sales.

Shipping

The single biggest reason for cart abandonment appears to be shipping costs. Some 46 percent of consumers surveyed by PayPal and comScore, said that they did not complete an online transaction because the shipping charges were too high. I have always recommended that etailers build the cost of shipping into the product price and/or have a low flat rate charge for shipping.

This lets consumers know up front what the final cost will be, greatly reducing the number of lost sales. If you are going to learn anything from Amazon, it should be to provide free shipping (either in the form of a membership site like Amazon Prime, or a minimum purchase amount like $35 as Amazon does).

Here's an example: I recently purchased a pair of mountain bike tires on eBay for $5 each. It sounded like a great deal until you read the shipping price: $17. That meant I could go buy the tires locally for the same cost. But, the ad stated, if I bought more than one item, the shipping would be combined and I could save substantially. OK, I thought, I'll buy a pair, and the shipping of the second item should only be a few dollars more and it will be worth it. Unfortunately, the way the eBay check out process works is that I didn't know what the total shipping for the combined purchase would be until after I had committed to buy. It turns out the cost of shipping the second tire was $14 (a whopping $3 savings!) Needless to say, I wasn't happy. This guy was making the tire look cheap, then making up for the price in shipping charges. That's a good way to lose people during the checkout process.

In fact, I have a customer who has been complaining that too many people abandoned their shopping carts on his website. The problem, according to this customer, is that the shipping costs are too high. (He uses real-time shipping calculations from UPS and charges the customer exactly what UPS charges him with no markup). Since I order stuff from him myself, and often pay $10 in shipping for a $10 item, I could see why his customers would be miffed and abandon their carts. So I made a suggestion to him: stop using real-time calculations from UPS. Instead, figure in the average shipping cost and add this to the price of his product. Then, advertise that he has free shipping. That way, there aren't any surprises during the check-out process and customers won't feel like they are getting ripped off. Instead, they'll feel like they got a great deal.

If your product is a physical one, then provide an option for 24 hour shipping. There's no one more demanding than a client whose waiting for their purchase; everyone wants everything—now. So gear yourself up accordingly and if necessary, charge a little extra.

Research shows that shipping costs are the number one reason for shopping cart abandonment. Sadly, the customer I mentioned above refused to consider my suggestion. If you really want a better conversion rate for people buying from your website however, you need to figure out how to do free shipping. Don't let the customer get away!

R—REQUEST AN ACTION

In the old world, you devoted 30% of your time to building a great service and 70% of your time to shouting about it. In the new world, that inverts.

—Jeff Bezos

there is an old adage in sales training that is abbreviated as ABC—Always Be Closing. This should apply to your Internet sales as well.

Statistics show that if you can get your customer to say "yes" at least eight times through trial closing questions then you will secure a sale! A trial question is one where the prospective buyer agrees with you on a series of smaller points. For example: If you had this online ordering system, wouldn't it help your resellers be able to place orders when you weren't available to answer the phone?

Your presentation should include a series of trial closing questions throughout the description and by including other requests for action on your product pages.

Most website designers will tell you that you shouldn't give your visitor too many options, or they don't know what they are supposed to click on—the extreme example is a squeeze page (a single page website where the only choice is to enter your email address to sign up, or leave the page). Often these type of pages follow the method of multiple trial close questions, which is why they work.

But unlike most websites today that are very clean, Amazon's pages are cluttered. The reason is that they are requesting for you to take an action—often multiple actions. Here are some of the types of actions you might request.

Cross-Sell

Once again, Amazon shines here, showing you what other customers purchased when they purchased the item you are looking at. They also show you alternative products that others purchased instead of the item you are looking at. And they will recommend accessories. This is known as cross-selling. For example, if you are looking at a "Kindle" (which just happens to be Amazon's best-selling product of all time), you might see:

And when you are looking at a product, such as Jana Mashonee's CD titled "American Indian Christmas", you will see a number of recommendations, including "Frequently Bought Together" and "Customers Who Bought This Item Also Bought":

Wishlist

Adding an item to a list for future purposes (and so Amazon can send you email reminders)

Product Reviews

Amazon asks if you own the product and would like to write a review about it.

Add to Cart

Ask for the order. This might be obvious, but you need to do more than just have an "Add to Cart" button. Just like in-person sales, ask buying questions and lead them down the path towards making a purchase. Experiment with different ways of doing this—instead of an "Add to Cart" button, try changing it to a "Get it Now" button and see which performs better for you.

Focus on getting your customers returning for repeated business. It is important that you are fully aware of how to promote your business to both new and existing customers, as this maximizes your profit per customer. If you keep your customer base happy, they'll return for more, so make sure they can contact you any time by email, because they may need to ask something about a product or purchase. A marketer who responds promptly with customers will make them feel better cared for than one who's only after their money.

Upsell

Vista Print is the king of asking for additional purchases—when you check out they are continually trying to upsell you (often for 5 or 6 pages before you can finally checkout, which is a little annoying). For example, if you purchase 500 business cards, during the checkout you are asked if you want letterhead and business envelopes, based on the same design. Then, even after you have checked out, they give you the opportunity to add additional business cards at a reduced rate if you add them to your order in the next 10 minutes. Brilliant!

+ PLUS: ADDITIONAL TIPS & SECRETS

"I very frequently get the question: 'What's going to change in the next 10 years?' And that is a very interesting question; it's a very common one. I almost never get the question: 'What's not going to change in the next 10 years?' And I submit to you that that second question is actually the more important of the two—because you can build a business strategy around the things that are stable in time."

—Jeff Bezos

amazon displays suggestions on its homepage based upon your past purchases and search history and then looks at what others have bought based on those patterns. Google displays search results based upon your physical location and your past searches. Facebook displays a newsfeed to you based upon who your friends are, what pages you've liked, combined with which of stories are the most popular. All of these provide a personal experience just for you.

As you look over these final tips and secrets, think about how you can make your customer's experience personal, and how you can use others to help you sell and market your products.

P –Perform Analytics

While this part of the equation is not as publically visible as other things Amazon does, you can be assured that they measure everything they do—and you should too. There are a number of tools that can help you do this.

Google Analytics

Google Analytics is the most well-known tool for measuring your website's performance, and you should absolutely be using it. There are other analytics programs available as well, and it is possible to use more than one analytics program. However, the data between the two may not be identical, so don't get hung up on how one program says one thing while Google Analytics says another—you need to be concerned with trends over time more than anything else. For this reason, a single analytics program will suffice, and Google is the best one. To create a Google Analytics account visit: http://www.google.com/analytics/

Once there, click on the "Admin" tab, then click on "Create New Account". If you already have other active accounts, click on the drop down list of accounts to find "Create New Account". Enter in the required information, and click on "Get Tracking ID". Your tracking ID will be in the format of: UA-11111111-1.

Next, find the link that says "Get Tracking Code". This will be a piece of JavaScript code that you need to install on your website. (That's how Google is able to keep track of everything). Put this in the footer of your site to it appears on every single page. If you are unsure how to do this, have your webmaster do it for you.

One of the things that Google Analytics measures is bounce rate. The bounce rate refers to how often someone, after entering your website, clicks the back button on their browser to go back to where they were. High bounce rates on their own are not necessarily a bad thing. Much depends on two other factors:

- What your bounce rate is like compared to your competitors?
- How long does it take before a visitor bounces? (Time to Bounce)

Most websites have a bounce rate between 40-60%. Per Alexa. com, Amazon's bounce rate is 28%. The daily page views per visitor is a little over 11 pages per visitor, and the average visitor is spending 9 minutes and 17 seconds on the site. How do your numbers compare to these? Google Analytics will measure these things for you.

If you have a WordPress website, I recommend installing the "Web-Ninja Google Analytics" or "Google Analytics Dashboard" plugin so you can view these statistics from your administrative dashboard without having to login to Google Analytics to see how you are performing. Here is an example of what you would see on your dashboard:

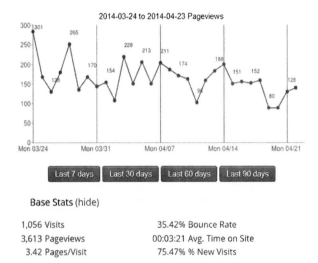

Base Stats (hide)

1,056 Visits	35.42% Bounce Rate
3,613 Pageviews	00:03:21 Avg. Time on Site
3.42 Pages/Visit	75.47% % New Visits

What Others are Saying…

Measuring the impact of social media is difficult, especially assigning hard data to its effectiveness. However, there are some sites out there that help you visualize how you are doing. If you monitor these sites over a period of time, it can help you determine which social media platforms perform the best for you.

Social Mention

SocialMention.com is a social media search and analysis site that aggregates user generated content from across the Internet into a single stream of information. It allows you to easily track and measure what people are saying about you, your company, a new product, or any topic across the web's social media landscape in real-time. Social Mention monitors 100+ social media properties directly including: Twitter, Facebook, YouTube, Digg, and Google. You can also use Social Mention to see how your competitors are doing with their social media campaigns.

Klout

Klout.com is a website that uses social media analytics to rank its users according to online social influence via the "Klout Score", which is a numerical value between 1 and 100. In determining the user score, Klout measures the size of a user's social media network and correlates the content created to measure how other users interact with that content. Klout uses Twitter, Facebook, Google+, LinkedIn, Foursquare, Wikipedia, and Instagram data to create Klout user profiles that are assigned a unique "Klout Score." Businesses can have a Klout account as well as individuals. While not perfect, this does give you an idea over time as to how well your social media campaigns are performing.

Google Alerts

Google Alerts is a content change detection and notification service, offered as a free service by Google. What this means is that whenever anyone posts anything about your company, you can get an instant notification via email so that you can respond to it. With everyone out there saying whatever they want about your company on Twitter, Blogs, Yelp, etc., you want to have a firm handle on this situation. Google Alerts is the best way to do this. Sign up for Google Alerts at: http://www.google.com/alerts

Email Analytics

Do you know what percentage of your emails get opened and read? How many people actually click on the links in your email?

A good bounce rate for emails is less than 5%. You can improve your email bounce rate by not sending emails to purchased or rented lists, clearing out old email addresses, and not sending to emails that already bounced. In other words—keep your email list clean and up to date.

Many email service providers include some form of email analytics in their offerings, although they may not give you all the data you need. The Wysija (now Mail Poet) plugin for WordPress is an email newsletter module that keeps track of who opened your email, who clicked on the email, and who unsubscribed. Here is an example:

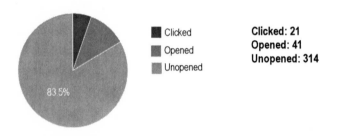

376 emails sent 1 day ago

This shows that 13% of the emails were opened, and 5% actually clicked on the link in the email. If you view the entire report, you can even see who the people were that opened and/or clicked on the email.

Litmus.com (among others) offers email analytics software to provide you with data you won't get from your email software. They work with your email service provider including Constant Contact and Mail Chimp by providing you with a small piece of HTML code that you insert into your email. You can then track all sorts of interesting things about your email including:

- Who actually read your email? Just because someone opened your email doesn't mean they read it. Break down your open rate to tell you how many people deleted your email, compared to how many read it.

- What device or email client did they use? Track the email client usage across your mailing lists, whether it be Outlook, Apple Mail, iPhone, Gmail or other.

- Did they forward or print your email? Track natural prints and forwards—right when your subscriber hits the button in the mail client—not those done via a web form. Track how many coupons got printed, or who shares your content most frequently.

- Where were they when they opened? Identify where your subscribers are around the world. Where should you host your next user group? Which time zones are most important? Have you considered content in other languages?

Tie email behaviors and data directly back to individual subscribers on your mailing list. Use this to segment, target and optimize. Use your data to identify customers that use their iPhone regularly and send them a targeted message regarding your upcoming app. Or send a content-rich newsletter to your most engaged subscribers. Segment your list in ways you never thought were possible.

Sales Analytics

This is really the bottom line. You might have all kinds of people visiting your site, very low bounce rates, great social mentions, and lots of people opening your emails, but the real test of your website's performance is if you are selling anything, either online or by driving people into your physical store. Do you have a way to track and measure this? Your eCommerce software should provide you with these reports.

Most small businesses can tell you what their best-selling product is, and some can even tell you how much it costs them to acquire the materials, produce the product, market the product, and ship it. Doing this for every product you sell is critical, so you can determine which products are making you money. Don't make the mistake of trying to use your website to discard non-performing products. Use your website to promote your best performing products.

L—Listen to your Customers

Online success comes from listening to what your customers want. Are your customers asking for free shipping? Are they asking to purchase your products on their mobile devices? Do they want the ability to find you on various marketplace sites (like an online mall)? Do they want a money back guarantee? 24x7 Support? How are you going to provide these things and remain competitive? One way you can do this is through a subscription program.

Subscription Programs

When you check out on Amazon, they attempt to upsell you with a subscription program they call "Amazon Prime." At the time of this writing, membership in Amazon Prime is $79 per year (it is about to go up). What this buys you is free shipping.

Customers spent as much as 150% more at Amazon after they become Prime members. Subscribers not only order more often, but after paying the $79 fee, they started buying things at Amazon that they probably wouldn't have in the past.

The net result of Prime membership — and the thing that has to scares Amazon's competition — is that it tends to cause subscribers to stop shopping anywhere else. It's assumed that Amazon's prices are competitive. With Prime, shipping costs become a total non-issue. Subscribers automatically defer to shopping at Amazon first because they know shipping is free.

A Prime member now makes $1,224 in Amazon purchases each year, on average, compared with $505 for non-Prime customers. After factoring in costs incurred for shipping and streaming, the average Prime member yields Amazon $78 more in profits than other customers, nearly equal to that $79 membership fee.

Does offering a "prime" membership where your customers pre-pay for a year's worth of free shipping make sense for your company? If not, what else can you offer your customers in the form of a membership site that will increase your revenues?

There are many different kinds of subscription service options that you can implement in your eCommerce site. You can also offer subscription pricing for a variety of products- from a single, full size item to a package of many disposable or consumable items. Consider the following subscription techniques:

- Offer a subscription service for "everyday items" that will easily appeal to customers who already regularly buy or use a product. Let them choose how often to have products sent to them and market this as an easy and practical option.
- Becoming increasingly popular for online shoppers are the monthly or periodic surprise and sample boxes. From beauty products to dog treats, there are many specific items that customers would love to subscribe to! This method also gives you the chance to introduce a wide range of products to customers who would have never tried them otherwise.

- A third subscription option, with a more targeted approach, is a membership pricing model which both attracts and earns regular customers by offering them exclusive discounts on your products or access to exclusive products. This approach will give you regular visitors and boost brand loyalty!

A subscription service is truly a feature that can separate your online store from hundreds of similar eCommerce sites you compete with every day.

Selling on Amazon

If Amazon is so successful and I recommend that you copy them, why not just become a vendor and sell through Amazon instead of having my own website?

This is a fair question, and not unlike people asking me if you should have an eBay store instead of creating your own eCommerce website. So why not just have an Amazon store, or perhaps and Amazon store and an eBay store? Actually having both is a good idea, because it's kind of like letting someone else market and sell for you. (Sound familiar?) And if you are selling arts and crafts, you might want to create an ETSY store as well. Here are some reasons why you might want to do this:

1. Increased Sales

The chief draw of selling on marketplaces such as Amazon and eBay is the scale of their online presence. Amazon alone draws nearly 85 million unique monthly visitors—that's a heck of a lot of eyeballs! And those eyeballs can translate into higher sales volumes. According to an Amazon executive, sellers report an average 50% increase in sales when they join Amazon Marketplace.

2. Customer Acquisition

Nobody visits Amazon or eBay searching for your store. But they may be searching for—and discover—your products. Products they may not have discovered otherwise, or that they may have purchased from a competitor.

Once you've got a customer in the door, even if it is through a marketplace, you've got a chance to win repeat business through excellent service and fulfillment. This is especially the case if you're selling products in a category that encourages frequent, repeated purchases.

3. Marketplace Infrastructure

Marketplaces are all about strength in numbers. This is as true for online marketplaces as it is for real world examples like farmers' markets and shopping malls. The variety and all-in-one aspect of the marketplace can draw in lots of customers who prefer that kind of shopping experience. Online marketplaces also bring the additional layer of single-stream checkout and fulfilment support in order to create a seamless experience for buyers.

But, you should still have your own online shop. Even if you end up selling the bulk of your items through other venues, you need a place on the Internet you can call home. And as we've seen with both Google and Facebook giving us tools and then taking them away, you need a place where you are the one that controls the rules. Finally, you need a place where the transaction costs are as low as possible without giving up a percentage of the sale to someone else. I believe you still need a place where you can run your own affiliate program and post your own testimonials—in short you still need to control your own destiny.

Setting up Shop on Amazon

Since 2000, selling on Amazon has been helping individuals and businesses increase sales and reach new customers. Today more than 30% of total sales come from third-party selection. Amazon basically offers 2 plans: A professional plan which cost $39.95 per month plus other selling fees, and an individual plan which costs $0.99/sale plus other selling fees. If you are selling more than 40 items per month and are looking for top placement on product detail pages, you will want the professional plan. Here's how to create a seller account:

1. Click on "Your Account." You can find this option under your name on the top right-hand side of the page.
2. Click on "Your Seller Account." This option is at the top of the menu on the right of the page.
3. Click "Start Selling." This will take you to a new page where you can choose which type of seller you are. Click this option under "Individual Sellers" or "Professional Sellers," depending on the type of seller you are.
4. Type in the relevant information. The next page will take you to a page where you can write down your seller information, such as your credit card information, seller name, and billing address.
5. Verify your phone number. Just type in your phone number, press "Call now," and type the 4-digit pin you're given into your phone after you receive and automated phone call.
6. Click "Register and Continue." This should finish setting up your seller account.

U—Understanding Distribution Channels

When you are in business, it is important that you understand the entire life-cycle of the products you sell, and the costs involved in manufacturing and delivery of those products so you can best serve your customer and make a profit. Whether you are a wholesale manufacturer or distributor selling to the retailer, or the retailer ordering from the wholesale supplier in order to sell to the final consumer, you should understand how B2B or business to business transactions work. This section explains how an online wholesale ordering system can improve your bottom line.

B2B Wholesale Considerations

Many wholesalers today continue to have tradeshows and printed catalogs as the focus of their marketing—after all, they are in a relationship business and this is how they build a client list. This book is not going to try to convince you to stop attending tradeshows (although it might persuade you to put your catalog online and avoid printing costs). But the Internet CAN play an important part in your business, and even become the primary way that clients find you, communicate with you, and even order products from you. After all, you've seen other companies create successful online sales, so why not you?

Business-to-consumer (B2C) eCommerce trends get a lot of attention in trade journals and other publications. Business-to-business (B2B) companies are fundamentally different from B2C companies. Because of the attention paid to B2C in the news (as well as availability of products and services built around the consumer model), B2B leaders too often try to apply B2C strategies and tactics in their companies with disappointing, even disastrous results. B2B success requires a completely different paradigm.

While there are many practices that are transportable between B2B and B2C, (and some of these marketing tactics should be applied to the B2B world aggressively), some things simply won't work. For example, points and "gamification" may represent a conflict of interest and be forbidden by the purchasing organization.

I often use the term "wholesale suppliers" rather than the more popular "B2B". This is done on purpose. B2B, or business to business refers to any transaction between businesses regardless of whether or not the purchaser intends to re-sell the goods and services, or simply consume them. For example, if my business purchases paper and toner cartridges from BestBuy, this is considered B2B, even though I intend to use the printing supplies myself. If I purchase a high enough quantity, I might even get a volume discount or "wholesale pricing", but ultimately, it is my company that is still consuming the goods. In fact, one definition that I've seen for the term "B2B" states:

> *"Businesses sell products and services to other businesses for use in their daily operations or for making other products and services."*

That clearly leaves out what I am primarily talking about—wholesale operations that sell to retailers for the specific purpose of reselling products to the final consumer.

Every state in the United States requires that businesses that sell at wholesale must have valid reseller permits for its customers, proving that sales tax will be collected at the retail level. Because they sell to the general public and collect sales tax, warehouses like Costco are not wholesale stores—they are simply large volume retailers.

The vast majority of eCommerce shopping carts on the market have the same mindset. They assume that the purchaser is the consumer, even if they are labeled B2B. I have approached this writing from the standpoint that the seller of goods and services has a client base of resellers—thus the term, "wholesale suppliers". A wholesale supplier might be a manufacturer, an importer, a distributor, or a grower of trees and shrubs. They do not typically engage in selling to end users—they are at the top of a distribution chain that sells to retailers, contractors and other middle men.

The online shopping experience for retailers purchasing from wholesalers is vastly different, yet many eCommerce software companies try to force consumer-oriented shopping carts on wholesale businesses when they simply aren't designed for the complexities of a B2B transaction. This has caused many wholesale suppliers to implement informational-only websites because the options available to them don't provide a solution to their needs. Still, there are good reasons to embark upon a B2B eCommerce system.

If you are a wholesale supplier, the single biggest reason to have an online ordering system and not just an informational website is so that your resellers can do business with you at their convenience. This alone should justify the cost of building a wholesale eCommerce website and will increase your revenues. But you will also save time by allowing your resellers to service themselves, such as checking on the status of an order.

Certainly, the Internet has collapsed this supply chain for many markets, and manufacturers may now sell to end users, eliminating the middle man. But for many markets, this is still in-efficient. Even a very large company is still likely to purchase paper from an office supply store rather than directly from Georgia-Pacific.

If you are sitting on the fence over whether or not to launch a business-to-business (B2B eCommerce site for your organization, it's time to stop thinking about B2B eCommerce and start doing something about it. Why? Simple. The potential market for your products via eCommerce is huge. Not big. Huge.

In their report, US Online Retail Forecast, 2011 to 2016, Key Trends in B2B eCommerce for 2013, Forrester Research, Inc. estimated that in 2013 B2C eCommerce will generate $252 billion in revenue. In the same time period, B2B eCommerce is estimated to generate $559 billion in revenue. That means the B2B eCommerce opportunity is more than twice the size of the B2C opportunity. (This includes businesses consuming goods for their own use, not just resellers). Interestingly, most B2B organizations don't have a viable eCommerce presence yet.

This means that when you launch your eCommerce site or move to your second generation eCommerce site, you will be ahead of your competition. This book will help you get there.

Highly successful B2C sites have raised customer experience expectations—including in the B2B space. In the past, companies tended to focus on creating a compelling customer experience for their B2C audience, treating B2B as an afterthought. Companies that insist on engaging the B2B buyer with traditional shopping carts will simply drive business to competitors who are ready and willing to provide updated tools. Given the revenue opportunities B2B represents and the fact that B2B customers are also exposed to B2C standards in their role as consumers, savvy B2B eCommerce teams are raising the bar, building new B2B sites to provide a better experience and investigating new ways to use Internet marketing.

Now a thoroughly mature industry on the B2C side, eCommerce is taking on an increasingly prominent role in B2B sales as well. As attractive as B2B online sales are, channel conflict remains a big concern for many companies. However, it should not be a roadblock. Top companies are leading the way by using eCommerce to benefit the direct business buyer experience—from enabling specific customer segments, to arming sales reps with online sales portals.

The worldwide wholesale distribution industry is going through a period of remarkable top-line revenue growth. Total sales of wholesale distributors continue to increase, once again discrediting forecasts of widespread disintermediation and the so-called "death of the middleman." Over-hyped developments, such as B2B exchanges, failed to displace wholesale distributors from their role as valuable service providers in the supply chain.

One of the reasons is that the wholesale supplier buying and selling experience is considerably more complicated than your typical B2C consumer experience. The shopping cart software needed by wholesale suppliers cannot just be the same cart as a retail store with "quantity discounts" thrown in. This is the reason why I developed the WebStores Ltd shopping cart as a wholesale-only cart.

Pricing models are different from one industry to the next, and sometimes even within the same industry. For example, wholesale jewelers sell product by the piece or by weight. Wholesale fabrics are priced by the yard. Soils are priced by the cubic yard or by the bag. Lumber by board feet. And on top of this, there are often an unlimited number of discount levels depending upon frequency of buying, amount purchased, credit rating, billing cycles, commitment levels, etc. You get the idea—the sales and distribution models of wholesalers is often more complex than a typical retailer. As a result, most B2B companies do not allow online purchasing without the involvement of a sales representative.

Here are a few ways that B2B transactions are different and how you need to address these on your website (based on the WebStores Ltd wholesale ordering system).

Unlimited Pricing Levels

Create an unlimited number of pricing levels and assign customers to the appropriate level. Each customer level can have different pricing and different payment terms based on commitment levels, frequency of purchases, and minimum purchase requirements.

Pay on Business Account

Wholesale customers don't buy with a personal credit card. You need to allow customers to charge to their Business Account with a company Purchase Order that is billed to their account. Customers should be able to make online payments to their account with echecks as well as credit cards.

Import Products

Since wholesale sites might have thousands of products, you need to be able to import or update those products all at once using a tab-delimited text file (Excel compatible).

Edit Orders

For various reasons, a customer may order something that requires a substitution. You may need to change an order even after it has been placed, allowing for back-ordered products and partial shipments.

Saved Orders

Enable customers to create saved orders so they can place weekly / monthly stocking orders with just a few clicks.

Minimum Orders

Set minimum order requirements by item and/or entire order for each price level.

Add Multiple Items at Once

Wholesale customers don't shop one item at a time like retail customers do. They want to simply fill out an order form. You must allow customers to add multiple products to the cart at once with Express Ordering or Table grid layout.

Coupons by Price Level

Offer different incentives for your best customers.

Persistent Cart

Wholesale orders can be complex and take time to complete. If the customer gets interrupted for any reason, they can return to where they left off.

Time Sensitive Banners & Boxes

The WebStores Ltd shopping cart allows you to create ads and promotional displays based on dates and price levels and display appropriately for the time of year. In fact, you can display different banners and different boxes so that your homepage (or any page) is a unique experience for one group of customers versus another.

Customizable

Every business has its own unique needs, especially at the wholesale level. You need a solution that can be modified to fit your needs. Since the WebStores Ltd online ordering system is customizable, think of how this could apply to your business. For example, instead of just price level—specific banners and boxes, why not take this a step further and create customer—level banners and boxes that are personalized to each visitor to your site (like Amazon does!)

Many organizations still waiver at the idea of implementing B2B eCommerce capabilities because of the common, yet misguided perception that the technical limitations and operational roadblocks involved are just too great to overcome. It's important to understand that B2B eCommerce goes beyond providing partners a web-based form and a few Marketing Materials in PDF format.

Taking orders online instead of by phone, e-mail, or fax, is a transformation that most wholesalers and manufacturers are either planning for, or going through these days. And they should, because online order taking is usually more cost effective than more 'traditional' ways of handling transactions. Perhaps more important: a good webstore will also boost your sales, since you have much more possibilities to promote specific products, leading to cross- and upsells, and also simply by the fact that you can take orders 24/7.

One of the challenges in successfully launching a (B2B) webstore (or also called online order portal), is to not only set it up, but also make sure that it's being adopted by your customers. Here are a few suggestions that will help you be successful in this:

- Promote your online order portal.
  This might sound so basic, but I see many cases in which
  a large part of the customers do not even know that
  they can order online. So when launching your online
  sales portal, consider doing a marketing campaign, or
  a launching event. And make sure you keep promoting
  your webstore, because like everything in marketing
  you need to repeat your message to make it stick. Email

marketing is a great way to promote your online order portal and remind customers that used it once, but might have forgotten about. You can also use email marketing to keep your customers up to date on new developments of the webstore.

- If customers order by phone, play a short message telling them that they can order online.
  Of course you want to offer your customers the possibility to order the way they like: by phone, fax, e-mail, or online. But for you, online orders will save time and money. So there is no harm in informing the customers that are calling you to place an order that they can also order online from now.

- Offer rewards if customers order online.
  Since the customers that place their orders online take work out of the hands of your sales force, you might consider some sort of reward, or incentive for this group of customers. This could be in the form of a discount, but could as well be something small to express your appreciation for working with you in this way.

- Make sure your webstore is really easy to use.
  According to a HubSpot survey, 76% of website visitors want a site where it is really easy to find what they are looking for—this includes both navigation and the search feature. Do not compromise on the ease of use with your online ordering system! You only have one chance to make a first impression with your customers, and if they do not like it from the first use, you will have a hard time convincing them to try again.

- Make sure customers don't have to search for their login information.

Not being able to login is one of the major reasons for customers not to use a suppliers' ordering portal again. So make it easy to recover, or reset their password if they do not have it at hand. And why not use their email address for login? Everybody will prefer that over some sort of client ID that is impossible to remember.

S—Start Now!

"Work hard, have fun, make history"

—Jeff Bezos

By reading this book you've learned that the secret to online success is to let other people market and sell products for you. You've seen how Amazon has accomplished this with affiliate marketing for driving traffic and using user reviews to convince others to buy their products. You saw how product descriptions and cross-selling were important in getting someone to buy your products. You've seen how effective email is and how you can grow your list with the help of others. You've learned how YouTube can increase your visibility and how a free offer can go viral.

But now you have a choice to make. You can read this information and simply tuck it away as knowledge to draw on. Or you can take action now.

To take action now, scan the QR code or visit:

www.AmazonsDirtyLittleSecrets.com

Many of the techniques described in this book can be outsourced with services from WebStores Ltd. Visit WebStoresLtd.com for details or call 877-924-1414.

I hope you have found this book valuable. If I have caused you to think about your marketing in a new way, I would appreciate a positive review on Amazon.com. I appreciate the time you have taken to read this. Remember, as you work on your website and your Internet marketing, don't forget to ask yourself, "What Would Jeff Do?"

ABOUT THE AUTHOR

 Greg Jameson is a Colorado Small Business of the Year and Inc 500 Award Winning Entrepreneur. He has spoken to audiences around the world about software solutions. His first book on eCommerce, "Grow Your Online Sales" was published in 2010.

What makes Greg Jameson qualified to write about eCommerce solutions? For starters, he is a software expert, having developed three commercial software applications, all of which remain on the market today. His first product, a landscape design program that worked with AutoCAD, was sold through a dealer channel nationally and a distribution channel internationally in over 20 countries.

Since the advent of the Internet, he has been designing or managing hundreds of websites. He has also been selling through an online store in the B2C space (CyberbaseTradingPost.com), working the other end of the spectrum and dealing with a number of suppliers, manufacturers and drop-shippers. His current software, the WebStores shopping cart is designed from the ground up as a B2B shopping cart.

He continues to be the creative force at WebStores Ltd., developing applications that are now used by thousands of businesses all over the world.

APPENDIX—COMPLETE LIST OF GOOGLE RANKING FACTORS

Here is a list of items that Google uses in its algorithm to determine how your page ranks and where it is displayed in the search results. Google uses about 200 factors to determine the ranking of your page (notice I said page, not site—Google ranks individual pages, not websites. Your goal should be to get every page on your site indexed by Google. Because Google keeps its algorithm secret, this is not an official list— much of this information was developed from an infographic created by AllTop.com and modified with commentary from personal experience.

It is not necessary to understand and implement everything on this list to get listed on page one of Google. Unless you are a web development professional, feel free to skip directly to the summary section at the end of this chapter to discover the dirty little secrets of search engine optimization.

Domain Factors

Domain age—how long your domain has been around, the longer the better.

Keyword appears in top level domain—for example, JoesCommercialPhotography.com if the keyword you are trying to rank for is "Commercial Photography". Not as relevant as it used to be, but still a factor.

Keyword as first word in domain—Commercial PhotographyByJoe.com instead of JoesCommercialPhotography.com

Domain registration length—make sure your domain name has been paid for for at least the next year, 5 years is better.

Keyword in subdomain name—such as photography.JoesGraphics.com

Domain history—a domain that has had a single owner rather than transferring ownership frequently is considered more stable.

Exact Domain Match—if someone is searching for "Joe's Commercial Photography", and your site is name "JoesCommercialPhotography.com", this gives you an edge.

Public versus Private WhoIs registration—private registration may be a sign of "something to hide".

Penalized WhoIs owner—if the site's owner has been marked as a spammer, this can downgrade your site.

Country TLD (Top Level Domain) extension—MySite.CA (Canada) may help you rank for that country, but may limit your visibility globally.

Page-Level Factors:

Keyword in Title Tag—The title tag is the page's second most important content (besides the page content itself) and sends a strong relevancy signal.

Title Tag Starts with Keyword—start your title tag with your keyword rather than using it later in the tag

Keyword in Description Tag—Yes, Google still uses the description tag. The "keyword" tag is now obsolete.

Keyword appears in H1 tag—The H1 (primary heading) tag can send a strong signal to Google about what your page should rank for.

Keyword is most frequently used word on the page—Try to use the keyword you are attempting to rank for at least 3 times on the page content and more often than any other words used on the page.

Content Length—Pages with longer content are preferred over shorter pages.

Keyword Density—Not as important as it once was and going overboard can hurt you, but you still want to use your most important keywords more often than other words on your page.

Latent Semantic Indexing (LSI) Keywords—if your keyword can have more than one meaning, such as Apple the computer company versus the fruit, having LSI keywords to explain the content can help.

LSI Keywords in Title and description Tags—as with webpage content, LSI keywords in a pages Meta data probably help Google with synonyms.

Page Loading Speed via HTML—Both Google and Bing use loading speed as a ranking factor.

Duplicate Content—Identical content on the same site, even slightly modified, but on different pages can negatively influence a site's search engine visibility.

Rel=Canonical—Used properly, this tag can prevent Google from considering pages to be duplicate content.

Page Loading Speed via Chrome—Since Chrome is a Google product, they may use this for testing non-HTML speed of your site.

Image Optimization—this includes file size, name, alt text, title, description, and caption.

Recency of Content Updates—Google favors recently updated content, especially for time-sensitive searches. In other words, frequently updated blogs are favored over static pages.

Magnitude of Content Updates—the significance of edits and changes is also a freshness factor. Adding or removing entire sections is a more significant update than switching around the order of a few words. Google prefers "fresh" sites.

Historical Updates Page Updates—How frequently does the page get updates? Daily? Weekly? Frequency of page updates also plays a role in freshness.

Keyword Prominence—Having a keyword appear in the first 100 words of a page's content appears to be a significance relevancy signal.

Keyword in H2, H3 Tags—Having your keyword appear as a subheading in H2 or H3 format may be another weak relevancy signal.

Keyword Order—An exact match of a searcher's keyword in a page's content will generally rank better than the same keyword phrase in a different order.

Outbound Link Quality—Many SEOs think that linking out to authority sites helps send trust signals to Google. This is probably a very minor factor, especially compared to inbound links.

Outbound Link Theme—According to SEOmoz, search engines may use the content of the pages you link to as a relevancy signal. For example, if you have a page about cars that links to a page about movie-related pages, this may tell Google that your page is about the movie Cars, not the automobile.

Grammar and Spelling—Proper spelling and grammar is a quality signal.

Syndicated Content—Is the content on the page original? If it's scraped or copied from an indexed page it won't rank as well as the original.

Helpful Supplementary Content—According to a leaked Google Rater Guidelines Document, helpful supplementary content is an indicator of a page's quality. Examples include currency converters, loan interest calculators and interactive recipes.

Number of Outbound Links—Too many dofollow OBLs may "leak" PageRank, which can hurt search visibility.

Multimedia—Images, videos, and other multimedia elements may act as a content quality signal.

Number of Internal Links Pointing to a Page—The number of internal links pointing to a page indicates it importance relative to other pages on a site.

Quality of Internal Links Pointing to a Page—Internal links from authoritive pages on a domain have stronger effect than pages with no or low PR.

Broken Links—Having too many broken links on a page may be a sign of a neglected or abandoned site. The Google Rater Guidelines Document uses broken links as one way to asses a homepage's quality.

Reading Level—Google estimates the reading level of webpages, but what they do with that information is up for debate.

Affiliate Links—Affiliate links themselves probably won't hurt your rankings, but if you have too many, Google's algorithm may pay closer attention to other quality signals to make sure you're not a "thin affiliate site".

HTML Errors / WC3 Validation—Lots of HTML errors or sloppy coding may be a sign of a poor quality website. However, easy to read code that is properly indented for human readability is not a factor—in fact there are programs to specifically remove all line feeds and modify variable names to make it harder for humans to read, yet browsers can render them just fine. This is known as encryption, which prevents people from stealing the code on your page. Encrypted pages do not affect page ranking, as Google's robots can read them, just like a browser can render them. Here is an example:

Original code:

```
//this function will calculate a factorial
function myFactorial(n)
{
/* we assume an integer input greater than or equal to zero */
if (n<=1) return 1;
var factorial_value=1;
var loop_index;
for (loop_index = 2; loop_index<=n; loop_index++)
{
factorial_value*=loop_index;
}
return factorial_value;
}
```

Encrypted code:

```
function x940202882765(x940202882766) { if
(x940202882766<=1) return 1; var x940202882767=1;
var x940202882768; for (x940202882768 = 2;
x940202882768<=x940202882766; x940202882768++)
```

```
{ x940202882767*=x940202882768; } return
x940202882767; }
```

Both the original and the encrypted code work equally well and do not affect page rankings.

JavaScript on Page—There are a lot of mixed messages out there when it comes to the topic of whether or not using JavaScript makes for good search engine optimization. The big attraction to JavaScript for web developers and designers is that it is a relatively simple programming language that can allow you to create many effects that traditional HTML simply cannot. In addition, JavaScript is a great solution to the problem of code bloat. Code bloat occurs when the size of an HTML file used for a web page approaches the limits set by the search engines. Exceed these limits, and you will be penalized with a lower ranking in the results pages.

However, there are plenty of critics out there who will tell you that using JavaScript can also harm your rankings, because it makes it harder for the search engines to crawl your site. The main reason people tend to look down on the use of JavaScript is that developers will often put navigation links inside JavaScripts. Since these links are invisible (hidden within the code) to the crawlers, they will not follow those links. Pages created by clicking on a "submit" button are not seen by search engines.

The best solution is to externalize your JavaScript code. Now, if you have only a few lines of JavaScript and a lot of keyword rich text on a given page, in all honesty, it probably won't affect your ranking enough to matter. But if you're going to incorporate a lot it, externalizing your JavaScript is definitely your best bet. All things considered, the use of JavaScript isn't going to make or break or break your page rankings.

Page Hosts Domain Authority—All things being equal a page on an authoritative domain will rank higher than a page on a domain with less authority.

Page's PageRank—Not perfectly correlated, but in general higher PR pages tend to rank better than low PR pages.

URL Path—A page closer to the homepage may get a slight authority boost.

URL Length—Search Engine Journal notes that excessively long URLs may hurt search visibility.

Keyword in the URL—another important relevancy signal. URL String—The categories in the URL string are read by Google and may provide a thematic signal to what a page is about. Google can (and does) index dynamically generated pages, but using words for categories and products can assist Google in determining what a page is about.

There is a popular misconception that dynamic URLs cannot be crawled. This is outdated thinking! Google claims it can crawl dynamic URLs and interpret the different parameters. About 10 years ago, most search engines would see a page that looked like: mysite.com/index.cfm?category=1&id=23 and as soon as the spider hit the "?" it would ignore anything after that, and you would only get index.cfm to be indexed by Google and not the individual pages. This has not been the case for many years, at least with Google. I believe this is one of the reasons why WordPress and other content management systems have become so popular. Per Google:

> *Much of the Internet is now dynamically generated, and being able to index that content effectively is one of the key factors in Google's success. Google will index your dynamic website or web application by following links to the dynamically*

generated pages. The dynamically generated pages will have
links to other dynamically generated pages, allowing Google
to "crawl" your dynamically generated content.

This is Google's official statement: *"Google now indexes URLs*
that contain the "&id=" parameter. So if your site uses a dynamic
structure that generates it, don't worry about rewriting it — we'll
accept it just fine as is."

If that is the case, why do we need to worry about "pretty
urls", changing the name of "mysite.com/?page_id=21? to "mysite.
com/services/"? The only real reason is for humans—computers
don't care.

Think about Amazon.com for a moment. Do you really think
that someone builds every page of the Amazon website in order to
get the search engines to crawl it? Of course not! Here is a typical
URL from Amazon:

http://www.Amazon.com/Canon-PowerShot-A2500-
Digital-2-7-Inch/dp/B00B5HE2UG/ref=sr_1_1?ie=UT
F8&qid=1382479467&sr=8-1&keywords=camera

The above URL is obviously both long and contains a number
(qid=) for coding purposes as well as the product name (for human
readability and perhaps SEO purposes), but this is also a very long
URL and it doesn't seem to hurt Amazon's pages from getting
indexed by Google.

Human Editors—Although never confirmed, Google has
filed a patent for a system that allow human editors to influence
the SERPs. In fact, for a while, searching for "Books" brought
up Google Books ahead of Amazon, making it clear that human
editors were tinkering with the results.

Page Category—The category the page appears on is a relevancy signal. A page that's part of a closely related category should get a relevancy boost compared to a page that's filed under an unrelated or less related category.

WordPress Tags—Google seems to like WordPress websites. Tags are WordPress-specific relevancy signals. According to Yoast. com: "The only way it improves your SEO is by relating one piece of content to another, and more specifically a group of posts to each other".

References and Sources—Citing references and sources, like research papers do, may be a sign of quality. The Google Quality Guidelines states that reviewers should keep an eye out for sources when looking at certain pages.

Bullets and Numbered Lists—Bullets and numbered lists can help break up your content for readers, making them more user friendly. Google likely agrees and may prefer content with bullets and numbers.

Priority of Page in Sitemap—the priority a page is given via the sitemal.xml file may influence ranking.

Too Many Outbound Links—straight from the aforementioned leaked document: "Some pages have way, way too many links, obscuring the page and distracting from the Main Content."

Quality of Other Keywords Page Ranks For—If the page ranks for several other keywords it may give Google an internal sign of quality.

Page Age—Although Google prefers fresh content, an older page that's regularly updated may out-perform a newer page.

User Friendly Layout—Citing the Google Quality Guidelines Document yet again: "The page layout on highest quality pages makes the Main Content immediately visible."

Parked Domains—a Google update in December 2011 decreased search visibility of parked domains.

Site-Level Factors:

Content Provides Value & Unique Insights—Google has stated that they are on the hunt for sites that don't bring anything new or useful to the table, especially thin affiliate sites.

Contact Us Page—The previously mentioned Google Quality Documents stats that they prefer sites with an "appropriate amount of contact information." Supposed bonus if your contact information matches your WhoIs info. While it doesn't affect your search rankings, it is good practice to include your phone number in the footer of every page of your website to let visitors know you are real and trustworthy to do business with.

Domain Trust / Trustbank—Site trust, measured by how many links away your site is from highly-trusted seed sites, is a massively important ranking factor. You can purchase "Trust Seals" from various companies, which help with human trust factors, but those seals do not affect Google's calculations.

Site Architecture—A well put together site architecture (especially a silo structure) helps Google thematically organize your content.

Site Updates—How often a site is updated, and especially when new content is added to the site, is a site-wide freshness factor.

Number of Pages—The number of pages a site has is a weak sign of authority. At the very least a large site helps distinguish it from thin affiliate sites. Squeeze pages (single page websites where the only option is to either enter your email or leave the page) are seen as undesirable by search engines as well.

Presence of Sitemap—A sitemap helps search engines index your pages easier and more thoroughly, improving visibility. You should have both a HTML sitemap (for humans) and an XML sitemap (for robots).

Site Uptime—Lots of downtime from site maintenance or server issues may hurt your ranking (and even result in de-indexing if not corrected).

Server Location—Server location may influence where your site ranks in different geographical regions, especially across international borders. This can influence geo-specific (local) searches).

SSL Certificate (Ecommerce Sites)—Google has confirmed that they index SSL (Secure Socket Layer) certificates. This is true with shared certificates as well. It stands to reason that they'll preferentially rank eCommerce sites with SSL certificates.

Terms of Service and Privacy Pages—These two pages help tell Google that a site is a trustworthy member of the Internet. Required by law in California.

Duplicate Content on-Site—Google will attempt to only index a single page on the same site with duplicate content, meaning that your other page may be ignored.

Breadcrumb Navigation—This is a style of user-friendly site-architecture that helps users (and search engines) know where they are on a site.

Mobile Optimized—Google's official stance on mobile is to create a responsive site. It's likely that responsive sites get an edge in searches from a mobile device. When searching from a non-mobile device, search results may be different, so if your users are looking for you on their cell phones, a mobile –responsive site is important.

YouTube—There is no doubt that YouTube videos are given preferential treatment in the SERPS (Search Engine Results Pages), probably because Google owns it. *This may be the most important thing you can do to get listed on page one of Google*—create a YouTube video that is properly tagged with the keywords you wish to rank for and link back to the page on your website that the video is about. You should also embed the video on that page.

Site Usability—A site that is difficult to use or to navigate can hurt ranking by reducing time on the site, pages viewed, and bounce rate. This may be an independent algorithmic factor gleaned from massive amounts of user data.

Use of Google Analytics and Google Webmaster Tools—Some think that having these two programs installed in your site can improve your page's indexing. This may also influence rank by giving Google more data to work with (i.e., more accurate bounce rate, whether or not you get referral traffic from your backlinks, etc.)

User Reviews / Site Reputation—A site's on review sites like Yelp.com and RipOffReport.com likely plays an important role in the algorithm. Google even posted a rarely candid outline of their approach to user reviews after an eyeglass site was caught ripping off customers in an effort to get backlinks.

Back-Link Factors:

Linking Domain Age—Links from aged domains may be more powerful than new domains.

# of Linking Root Domains—The number of referring domains is one of the most important ranking factors in Google's algorithm. To have this make an impact on your position though requires about 800 different domains pointing to your page.

# of Links from Separate C-Class IPs—Links from separate c-class IP addresses suggest a wider breadth of sites linking to you.

# of Linking Pages—The total number of Linking pages, even if some are on the same domain, is a ranking factor.

Alt Tag (for Image Links)—Alt text is an image's version of anchor text.

Links from .EDU or .GOV Domains—Top Level Doman extensions may not factor into a site's importance, but that doesn't stop SEOs from thinking that there's a special place in the algorithm for .gov and .edu domains.

PageRank (PR) of Linking Page—The PageRank of the referring page is an extremely important ranking factor. Also known as "the Oprah Effect", if an important page links to your page, that gives your ranking a huge boost.

Authority of Linking Domain—The referring domain's authority may play an independent role in a link's importance (i.e., a PR2 page link from a site with a homepage PR3 may be worth less than a PR2 page link from PR8 yale.edu).

Links from Competitors—Links from other pages ranking in the same SERP may be more valuable for a page's rank for that particular keyword.

Social Shares of Referring Page—The amount of page-level social shares may influence the link's value.

Links from Bad Neighborhoods—Links from "bad neighborhoods" may hurt your site.

Guest Posts—Links from guest posts, especially in an author bio area, may not be as valuable as a contextual link on the same page.

Links to Homepage Domain that Page Sits On—Links to referring page's homepage may play special importance in evaluating a site's (and therefore a Link's) weight.

NoFollow Links—One of the most controversial topics in SEO, Google's official word on the matter: *"In general, we don't follow them."* Which suggests that they do, at least in certain cases. Most likely, Google does follow them, but doesn't list the resulting page. Having a certain percentage of NoFollow links may also indicate a natural versus unnatural link profile.

Diversity of Link Types—Having an unnaturally large percentage of your links come from a single source (i.e., forum profiles, Blog comments) may be a sign of webspam. On the other hand, links from diverse sources is a sign of a natural link profile.

Contextual Links—Links embedded inside a page's content is considered more powerful than links on an empty page of found elsewhere on the page (i.e., the menu).

Sponsored Links or other words around the Link—Words like "sponsors", "link partners", and "sponsored links" may decrease a link's value. In Joel Comm's excellent book on AdSense, he discusses how links should appear to be part of the content rather than looking like an ad.

Excessive 301 Redirects to page—Links coming from 301 redirects dilute some (or even all) PR.

Backlink Anchor Text—The anchor text is the visible, clickable text in a hyperlink. The words contained in the anchor text can determine the ranking that the page will receive by search engines. As noted in this description of Google's original algorithm: *"First, anchors often provide more accurate descriptions of web pages than the pages themselves"*. In other words, a link that contains anchor text is more valuable than a link that just says www.MySite.com

Internal Link Anchor Text—Internal link anchor text (links from one page to another page on the same site), is another relevancy signal, but probably weighted differently than backlink anchor text.

Link Title Attribution—The link title (the text that appears when you hover over a link) is also used as a weak relevancy signal.

Country TLD (Top Level Domain) of Referring Domain—Getting links from country-specific top level domain extensions (i.e., .cn, .ca, .uk) may help you rank better in that country.

Link Location in Content—Links in the beginning of a piece of content carry slightly more weight than links placed at the end of the content.

Link Location on Page—Where a link appears on a page is important. Generally, links embedded in a page's content are more powerful than links in the footer or sidebar area.

Linking Domain Relevancy—a link from a site in a similar niche is significantly more powerful than a link from a completely unrelated site.

Page Level Relevancy—a link from a page that's closely tied to your niche is more powerful than a link from a page with content that has nothing to do with your site.

Text Around Link Sentiment—Not all publicity is good publicity. Google has probably figured out whether or not a link to your site is a recommendation or part of a negative review. Links with positive sentiments around them likely carry more weight.

Keyword in Title—Google gives extra love to links on pages that contain your page's keyword in the title (experts linking to experts).

Positive Link Velocity—A site with positive link velocity usually gets a SERP boost.

Negative Link Velocity—Negative link velocity can significantly reduce rankings as it's a signal of decreasing popularity.

Links from "Hub" Pages—Getting links from pages that are considered top resources (or hubs) on a certain topic are given special treatment.

Link from Authority Sites—A link from a site considered to be an "authority site" likely pass more juice than a link from a small, microniche site.

Linked to as Wikipedia Source—Although the links are "NoFollow", many think that getting a link from Wikipedia gives you a little added trust and authority in the eyes of search engines.

Co-Occurrences—The words that tend to appear around your backlinks helps tell Google what that page is about.

Backlink Age—According to a Google patent, older links have more ranking power than newly minted backlinks.

Links from Real Sites vs. Splogs—Due to the proliferation of Blog networks, Google probably gives more weight to links coming from "real sites" rather than from fake blogs. They likely use brand and user-interaction signals to distinguish between the two.

Internal or External Blog Links –It would make sense that a blogger site (which is owned by Google) would provide good link juice for your site, but Google usually stops paying attention after five links from the same website pointing to your page.

Natural Link Profile—A site with a "natural" link profile is going to rank highly and be more durable to updates.

Reciprocal Links—Google's Link Schemes page lists "excessive link exchanging" as a link scheme to avoid. This includes 3-way links as well as a 2-way trade.

User Generated Content Links—Google is able to identify links generated from User Generated Content (UGC) vs. the actual site owner. For example, they know that a link from the official WordPress.com Blog at en.Blog.wordpress.com is very different than a link from besttoasterreviews.wordpress.com. UGC is more powerful than links from the site owner.

Links from 301—Links from 301 redirects may lose a little bit of juice compared to a direct link, however some SEOs think that a 301 link is similar to a direct link.

Schema.org Microformats—Pages that support microformats may rank above pages without it. This may be a direct boost or the fact that microformatting may have higher SERP Click Through Rates.

DMOZ Listed—Many believe that Google gives DMOS listed sites a little extra trust. At the very least, it gives you another backlink and minor search engines may rely on DMOZ heavily.

Yahoo! Directory Listed—The algorithm might also have a special place for the Yahoo! Directory considering how long it has been cataloging sites. Now that Microsoft Bing own Yahoo!, this may diminish.

Number of Outbound Links on Page—PageRank is finite. A link on a page with hundreds of OBLs passes less PR than a page with only a few OBLs.

Forum Profile Links—Because of industrial-level spamming, Google may significantly devalue links from forum profiles.

Word Count of Linking Content—A link from a 1000-word post is more valuable than a link inside of a 25-word snippet.

Quality of Linking Content—Links from poorly written or spun content don't pass as much value as links from well-written, multimedia enhanced content.

Sitewide Links—Sitewide links are "compressed" to count as a single link. In other words, the same link multiple times on a site only give you the value of a single link.

User Interaction:

Organic Click Through Rate for a Keyword—Pages that get clicked more in Click Through Rates (CTR) may get a SERP (Search Engine Results Page) boost for that particular keyword.

Organic CTR for All Keywords—a page's (or site's) organic CTR for all keywords it ranks for may be a human-based, user interaction signal.

Bounce Rate—Bounce rate is the percentage of visitors to a particular website who navigate away from the site after viewing only one page. This includes robots. Not everyone in SEO agrees bounce rate matters, but it may be a way for Google to use their own users as quality testers (pages where people quickly bounce is probably not very good).

Direct Traffic—It's confirmed that Google uses data from Google Chrome to determine whether or not people visit a site (and how often). Sites with lots of direct traffic are likely higher quality than sites that get very little direct traffic. This means that bookmarked sites and email links are very important (and often drive the majority of your traffic as we'll discover in later chapters).

Repeat Traffic—Google may also look are whether or not users go back to a page or site after visiting. Sites with repeat visitors may get a SERP boost.

Blocked Sites—If you don't like a site that appears in your search results, Google used to have a feature that allowed you as an individual to block that site from appearing in your results. Sites would only be blocked for you, but Google would use that data to improve ranking of search results for everyone. This feature has been discontinued.

Chrome Bookmarks—People use all sorts of browsers including Internet Explorer, Firefox, and Safari. But we know that Google collects Chrome browser usage data. Pages that get bookmarked in Chrome might get a boost.

Google Toolbar Data—Search Engine Watch reports that Google uses toolbar data as a ranking signal. However, besides page loading speed and malware, it not known what kind of data they glean from the toolbar.

Number of Comments—Pages with lots of comments may be a signal of user-interaction and quality.

Time on Site—the longer a user remains on your site, the stronger the signal that this is a quality site, which plays into Google's ranking algorithm.

Special Algorithm Rules:

Query Deserves Freshness—Google gives newer pages a boost for certain searches.

Query Deserves Diversity—Google may add diversity to a SERP for ambiguous keywords such as "ted", "WTF" or "ruby".

User Browsing History—Sites that you frequently visit while signed into Google get a SERP bump for your searches. As a result, what you see may be different than what someone else sees.

User Search History—Search chain influence search results for later searches. For example, if you search for "reviews" then search for "toasters", Google is more likely to show toaster review sites higher in the SERPs.

Geo Targeting—Google gives preferences to sites with local IP addresses. A search for restaurants in Philadelphia will produce different results than the same search in Denver.

Safe Search—Search results with curse words or adult content won't appear for people with Safe Search turned on.

Google+ Circles—Google shows higher results for authors and sites that you've added to your Google Plus Circles. Since

Google Plus is a Google property, we can expect this to increase in importance over time.

DMCA Complaints—The Digital Millennium Copyright Act (DMCA) is a United States copyright law that implements two 1996 treaties of the World Intellectual Property Organization (WIPO). Google "downranks" pages with DMCA complaints.

Domain Diversity—The so-called "Bigfoot Update" supposedly added more domains to each SERP page. I found this to be true, as a search for "Greg Jameson" used to show only pages about me, now it shows others who also share my name.

Transactional Searches—Google sometimes displays different results for shopping-related keywords, like flight searches.

Local Searches—Google often places Google+ Local results above the "normal" organic SERPS.

Google News Box—Certain keywords trigger a Google News box.

Big Brand Preference—After the Vince Update, Google began giving big brands a boost for certain short-tail searches. Size does matter, even on the Internet.

Shopping Results—Google sometimes displays Google Shopping results in organic SERPS.

Image Results—Google elbows our organic listings for image results for searches commonly used on Google Image Search.

Single Site Results for Brands—Domain or brand-oriented keywords bring up several results from the same site.

SOCIAL SIGNALS:

Number of Tweets—Like links, the tweets a page has may influence its rank in Google.

Authority of Twitter Users Accounts—It's likely that Tweets coming from aged, authority Twitter profiles with a ton of followers (like Justin Bieber) have more of an effect than tweets from new, low-influence accounts.

Number of Facebook Likes—Although Google can't see most Facebook accounts, it's likely they consider the number of Facebook likes a page receives as a weak ranking signal.

Facebook Shares—Because these are more similar to a backlink, Facebook shares may have a stronger influence than Facebook Likes.

Authority of Facebook user Accounts—As with Twitter, Facebook shares and likes coming from popular Facebook pages may pass more weight.

Pinterest Pins—Pinterest is an insanely popular social media account with lots of public data. It's probable that Google considers Pinterest Pins a social signal.

LinkedIn Connections—Having a lot of connections appears to be one of the elements of profile page-ranking for Google.

Votes on Social Sharing Sites—It's possible that Google+ uses shares are sites like Reddit, StumbleUpon, and Digg as another type of social signal.

Number of Google+1's—Matt Cutts leads the Webspam team at Google, and works with the search quality team on search engine optimization issues. He has gone on record as saying that Google+ has "no direct effect" on rankings, but it's hard to believe that they would ignore their own social network when they obviously use others. In fact, several of the 10 most important factors in SEO ranking now come from social media, with Google +1s leading the way.

Authority of Google+ User Accounts—It's logical that Google would weigh +1's coming from authoritative accounts more than from accounts without many followers.

Verified Google+ Authorship—In February 2013, Google CEO Eric Schmidt famously claimed: *"Within search results, information tied to verified online profiles will be ranked higher than content without such verification, which will result in most uses naturally clicking on the top [verified] results."* Verified authorship may already be a trust signal.

Social Signal Relevancy—Google probably uses relevancy information from the account sharing the content and the text surrounding the link.

Site Level Social Signals—Site-wide social signals may increase a site's overall authority, which will increase search visibility for all of its pages.

Brand Signals:

Brand Name Anchor Text—Anchor text is the word used when creating a hyperlink. Branded anchor text is a simple, but strong, brand signal. In spite of how people have said that the Internet levels the playing field, big brands do have an advantage over small businesses.

Branded Searches—It's simple: people search for brands. If people search for your site on Google, they likely take this into consideration when determining a brand.

Site has Facebook Page and Likes—Brands tend to have Facebook pages with lots of Likes.

Site has Twitter Profile with Followers—Twitter profiles with a lot of followers signals a popular brand.

Official LinkedIn Company Page—Most real businesses have company LinkedIn pages.

Employees Listed at LinkedIn—Having LinkedIn profiles that say they work for your company is a brand signal.

Legitimacy of Social Media Accounts—A social media account with 10,000 followers and 2 posts is probably interpreted differently than another 10,000 follower strong account with lots of interaction.

Brand Mentions on News Sites—Really big brands get mentioned on Google News sites all the time. In fact, some brands even have their own Google News feed on the first page.

Co-Citations—Brands get mentioned without getting linked to. Google likely looks are non-hypertext brand mentions as a brand signal.

Number of RSS Subscribers—Your Blog has a feed known as Real Simple Syndication or RSS where people can subscribe to your posts. Brands have lots of RSS subscribers.

Brick and Mortar Location with Google+ Local Listing— Real businesses have offices. It's possible that Google fishes for location-data to determine whether or not a site is a big brand.

Website is a Tax paying Business—SEOmoz reports that Google may look at whether or not a site is associated with a tax-paying business.

On-Site Webspam Factors:

Panda Penalty—Sites with low-quality content (particularly content farms) are less visible in search after getting hit with a Panda Penalty.

Links to Bad Neighborhoods—Linking out to "bad neighborhoods", like pharmacy or payday loan sites, may hurt your search visibility.

Redirects—Sneaky redirects is a big no-no. If caught, you can get a site not just penalized, but de-indexed.

Popups or Distracting Ads—The official Google Rater Guidelines Document says that popups and distracting ads is a sign of a low-quality site.

Site Over-Optimization—Includes on-page factors like keyword stuffing, header tag stuffing, and excessive keyword decoration.

Page Over-Optimization—many people report that, unlike Panda, Penguin targets individual pages (and even then just for certain keywords).

Ads Above the Fold—The "Page Layout Algorithm" penalizes sites with lots of ads (and not much content) on the page without having to scroll.

Hiding Affiliate Links—Going too far when trying to hide affiliate links (especially with cloaking) can bring on a penalty.

Affiliate Sites—It's no secret that Google isn't the biggest fan of affiliates. And many think that sites that monetize with affiliate links are put under extra scrutiny.

Auto-Generated Content—Google isn't a big fan of auto-generated content. If they suspect that your site is pumping out computer-generated content, it could result in a penalty or de-indexing.

Excess PageRank Sculpting—Going too far with PageRank sculpting, by nofollowing all outbound links or most internal links, may be a sign of gaming the system.

IP Address Flagged as Spam—If your server's IP address is flagged for spam, it may hurt all the sites on that server.

Meta Tag Spamming—Keyword stuffing can also happen in Meta tags. If Google thinks you're adding keywords to your Meta tags to game their algorithm, they may hit your site.

Off-Page Webspam Factors:

Unnatural Influx of Links—A sudden (and unnatural) influx of links is a sure-fire sign of phony links.

Penguin Penalty—Sites that were hit by Google's Penguin update are significantly less visible in search.

Link Profile with High % of Low Quality Links—Lots of links from sources commonly used by black hat SEOs (like Blog comments and forum profiles) may be a sign of gaming the system.

Linking Domain Relevancy—The famous analysis by MicroSiteMasters.com found that sites with an unnaturally high amount of link from unrelated sites were more susceptible to Penguin.

Unnatural Links Warning—Google sent out thousands of "Google Webmaster Tools notice of detected unnatural links" messages. This usually precedes a ranking drop, although not 100% of the time.

Links from the Same Class C IP—Getting an unnatural amount of links from sites on the same server IP may be a sign of Blog network link building.

"Poison" Anchor Text—Having "poison" anchor text (especially pharmacy keywords like Cialis or Viagra) pointed to your site may be a sign of spam or a hacked site. Either way it can hurt your site's ranking.

Manual Penalty—Google has been known to hand out manual penalties, like in the well-publicized Interflora fiasco.

Selling Links—Selling links can most definitely impact toolbar PageRank and may hurt your search visibility.

Google Sandbox—The Sandbox is a name given to an observation of the way Google ranks web pages in its index. According to the theory of the sandbox effect, links which may normally be weighted by Google's ranking algorithm may be subjected to filtering to prevent their having a full impact. Some observations have suggested that two important factors for causing this filter to come into play are the active age of a domain, and the competitiveness of the keywords used in links.

Google Dance—Google Dance is a slang term used to describe the period of time in which Google used to rebuild its rankings, and as a result of this rebuilding, rankings of websites on Google's SERP may fluctuate in order during a several day period. This eventually died out, but returned in 2012. The Google Dance can temporarily shake up rankings. According to a Google Patent, this may be a way for them to determine whether or not a site is trying to game the algorithm.

Disavow Tools—Use of the Disavow Tool may remove a manual or algorithmic penalty for sites that were the victims of negative SEO.

Reconsideration Request—A successful reconsideration request can lift a penalty, but these are not easy to obtain.

INDEX